Caleb Klaces is the author of *Bottled Air* (Eyewear, 2013), which won the Melita Hume Poetry Prize and an Eric Gregory Award, and two chapbooks, *All Safe All Well* (Flarestack, 2011) and *Modern Version* (If a Leaf Falls Press, 2018). Extracts from *Fatherhood* won a 2015 Northern Writers Award. He teaches at York St John University.

Fatherhood
by Caleb Klaces

Fatherhood

The world we live in is a mistake, a clumsy parody.
Mirrors and fatherhood, because they multiply and
confirm the parody, are abominations.
  Jorge Luis Borges

This is the one world, bound to itself and exultant.
  Annie Dillard

In the tenth month of my wife's pregnancy I put aside my lifelong commitment to avoiding harm, and purchased mousetraps. The rodent population had exploded during spring, and now the summer was so hot that young mouse families were fleeing the plane trees' inadequate shade for the cool of the ancient riverbed which lay under the cellar of our rented basement flat. They emerged in our kitchen at night to lap at the spilled juice of the pineapple intended to entice our unborn child into the visible world.

Under the greasy sun, a fox made parenting look elegant. She licked her paws while three squealing cubs dug up a piece of black meat with four legs and a collar. Inside, we sat naked between mounds of bleached-white baby clothes and watched the World Cup. *All these men are alive*, I kept thinking. Layers of shadow billowed on neon turf. The players played on regardless.

My wife had a job. I had a grant to write a novel. A distant relative from the Russian branch of my family had died, unexpectedly leaving us a slice of the proceeds of his bedsit. The will stipulated that we use it to invest in a piece of England. I scrolled through photographs of farms and beach huts, unable to take myself seriously enough to consider a period terrace. When I imagined life outside of the capital, above ground, I already missed the city.

The feeling reminded me of the final summer of university: a blank stretch between exams and results, when everything is over and nothing has yet begun. Ten years before, we had shared an itch. We left our notebooks out for one another to read. After lunch we took pills and whispered about our social responsibilities. On the way from one pub to another we broke off from the group to find a bedroom, any bedroom.

Not since then had my wife and I been so physically involved. We were the only members of our group, but we snuck quietly to the bedroom. We drew the curtains on the watching fox.

This time the logistics—pillows, headboards—were confounding. We rolled away from one another and lay still. It was necessary, all of a sudden, to be polite to the baby. I took chocolate bars from the labour bag and we ate them in the dark. We dreamt we were too old to move.

But the next morning, we slotted together in ferocious agreement. I loved—I don't know how to say this—the feeling that I was drawing the baby out into the world, that my desire was extending a greeting, to which an unseen body might respond. There were so many pulses: in the throat and in the taut, round stomach; in the places where bodies curve into themselves, fold and open. Each of us pulsed with the blood of the others. I counted myself, counted myself again.

Do I need to lay down a bin bag?

I wanted to be the taxi driver's friend and I had
never seen my wife so powerful and so delicate
and I didn't know what to reply.

My wife, after eight hours of contractions,
was deep inside pain. I said no to the bin bags
and helped her into the taxi. I discovered that
I was a prude, flinching at the small moans
becoming public.

The breeze through the taxi window did
something wonderful. The contractions appeared to pause. She smiled. She looked like
a disco ball, glittering in daylight.

The driver said into his mirror that it was all
worth it. We thanked him.

Offensive speed bumps on the hospital roads.

I expected a welcome party. Instead I saw
midwives eating packed lunch on a wall. I said,

That's nice, midwives eating their
packed lunches.

The taxi driver hung all the bags and car seat
off his arms and followed us in. My wife found
the buzzer. She was back behind a cloud.

There was a chair so my wife sort of sat on it.
Every part of her was involved in the convul-
sions. The midwife took phone calls. I filled the
water bottle.

Let's get you onto the bed.
I can see baby's head.
Curtain across.
The midwife abandoned taking her pulse.

You've done very well to get to this point
on your own.

My wife had been courteous, I wanted to say,
since 5 a.m when she woke with contractions.
We had walked the contractions round the park,
under the dovecote, stopping at the toilets.
At home we had sat in darkness with the contractions while I asked her medium-difficulty
trivia questions. I had cleaned every fork in
the drawer and spent minutes choosing socks.
I wanted to be wearing the right pair of socks.
She had been in labour while I spent an hour
chasing a butterfly out of the window, refusing
the metaphor. She had been in labour while
I read online reviews of taxi companies. Now
I touched her shoulder and she thanked me and
asked me not to touch her shoulder.

We need to get you onto this bed.
Can I stay on this bed?
There's not enough room for two beds in
this room.
I can't move. Can I have a moment?
                                    (Astonishing poise.)

Take your time.

Gas and air. My wife lifted herself with great effort and lightly. A new midwife arrived, introducing herself as someone we had bumped into in the corridor. I said it was nice to finally meet her. The midwife angled the bed. Someone took the baby's heart rate.

Time started again, or events waited in line rather than happening all at once. I ran away towards where I was. I found the flannel—an unbelievable triumph—and doused it. My wife took it with a slow, steady hand. I breathed gas and air. I told her she could do it. Then I corrected myself to say that she was doing it. The midwife heard me and also said,

You are doing it.
You are doing it.

My wife apologised for the noise she was making. The whole room giggled with disbelief. I think I said,

It's a great noise!
It's a great noise!

A pause, as when waiting for a reply from someone who has left the room.

I stroked her face. Her eyes were wide and alarmed, making room for the baby the midwife was talking to, inside and outside the room:

Keep your heart beating for me.

Then asking everyone in the room
to push for
me for
the first time
too much
baby

slid into the midwife's arms. Slow and sudden as something missed. I had been crying for some time. I looked down towards where the baby would be. It was too much: the sun. Grey baby on a rope.

Grey sun seen through sobs. Grey baby, gulping towards a breast. There was beautiful purple thick blood on the sheets. I wanted to lay a hand on every head in the room. I wanted another word for love.

The midwife hovered between the machinery and us. She smiled, was about to say something, then returned to her task.

I didn't hold the baby immediately. The baby was all that I could see and was impossible to look at. I approached, then didn't. There was a soothing commotion around the end of the bed as the midwife gathered up bloody sheets. My wife smiled one long solid smile. She asked the baby,

What do you know, baby? Please tell us.

I rubbed my head against my daughter's head. I kissed my wife. I fell away again into my corner. I returned and kissed them both. I was surprised not to know who my daughter was.

Strange weightless conversation broke out then with the midwife, answers and questions spoken without conscious thought.

The placenta, the baby's only belonging, filled a bucket. Of which:

Do you want to take a photograph?

The baby arrives home. You must bathe it in words. You are a relentless tour guide, unfamiliar with the world you describe. The baby arrives at the home of its home, which is its mother's body. You care for its mother's body. There is nothing you do not want to take care of. You take care of a gin and tonic and dab the baby's head. You dream about the baby's head pickling in gin and tonic. When you wake, the baby is where you left it. You believe you can feel the movement of air when the moth lifts. You can taste the notes of kumquat promised by the coffee's packet. You are surely a good father. You cannot get enough of the midwife's praise for the quick birth, the breathing baby, her I HEART DAD mug of milky English Breakfast. Then the midwife starts telling you a story about a couple she worked with who unpicked the mother's stiches themselves—they stored them in a biscuit tin—so that they could return, post-haste, to their intimacy, and in your hyper-receptive state you think the midwife is trying to tell you something, but what?—that is, until she goes on to describe the exorcisms her husband performed when they lived down in the dark south-west, and it is clear she means no more than she means. You are still a good father. A good husband, too, she confirms. Intimacy between the two would-be parents, you now realise, had been stifled by a nervous desire for intimacy, as though the only way to be close was actually to enter one another. Before the baby, you see now, each touch had broken you into a new set of parts: your feet and your ears occupied different rooms, different tenses. To your surprise, the new body puts everything back together again in the present. The animal will not be apart from the family it has created. Time is coated in the animal, which goes on living as you go on. With the animal in the room it is necessary to wait for the next word before moving on to the word after that; a manner of speaking contrived to move at the tempo the baby keeps alive; not contingent on a particular past and not anticipating a particular future; only moving away from or towards being present as it continues, until forty-two days have sped by, at which point the parents of a child are legally obliged to register the name of the child and the child with a name with the crown. You watch with pride as the Registrar of Births and Deaths lifts a sheet of slightly green watermarked paper from a locked drawer and sends it through a gravely dustless desktop printer to print the name, sex, date of birth, place of birth (district and sub-district), her own name and jurisdiction and the present date, then signs the certificate, to make the baby official. You say to your official baby,

I won't fuck this up.

/

The technology to construct modern skyscrapers existed long before the skyscraper became modern; the problem was the number of stairs. Stepping would have replaced office work as the office workers' chief activity. Once the lift had released time into tall buildings it made its way into shorter ones, where more important than its production of time is its ability to render marginalised sections of society publicly visible. In a three-floor upmarket outlet one morning the lift doors had closed before either of two fathers, previously and still strangers both to one another and to the use of department store lifts, could assert control over bulky prams at the same time as the order in which they should exit. The lift, with them and their newborns inside their prams, was ascending. It shocked them both, the existence of another baby. Each father and pram was multiplied several times in the mirrored walls and the illusion appeared to extend back into the objects being reflected: each baby was repeated in a foreign pram. One baby broke the tension. It cried. The other baby didn't cry. The crying baby's father stroked the side of his baby's head, something he had never done before, a region beside the eye where he felt a circular patch of skin with more give, deep enough that he thought the word 'divot', not something he would consider part of his child unless he happened to stroke her there. With the first touch the baby's arms flew upwards. The other father's hand covered his jeans pocket, finding his keys before his mind had caught up with the hand's fear that the keys might not be in his pocket. The baby continued to cry, almost silently. A tear rose in the corner of its eye and burst down the side of its head. Until now the baby's father had only seen other people's tears run down her face. The way the tear made its glossy point seemed melodramatic, but he was genuinely wounded. He remembered standing above a river where it flowed underground on the outskirts of a city. The river continued under his feet with the clank of the lift. There was a grate over the entrance to the tunnel gathering detritus from the river, including a blow-up doll dressed in a sailor's outfit, perpetually drowning. The sight made him laugh in the same way that his baby's apparently desperate cries made him laugh. Both men, as they watched the baby's arms fall slowly down past its head, all the features of which were dragged into its red choking centre, became aware of the floor's movement upwards, as if it was travelling through their feet as well as the air. She doesn't like lifts, the father of the crying baby said to the father of the baby who was not crying, who replied, Sorry I thought she was a he. I did too. So did I. An expression of curiosity rippled across the silently crying baby's face, before it drained back into its centre, this time making noise. In response, and to finish the conversation before it began, two hands found their way through the sweaty layers of redundant blankets to pick up the baby. The baby's head jerked backwards as if snagged on the pram and her crying deepened to purple. She appeared to be eating each cry. Her head hit her father's jaw. Her toes raked down his chest. He had recently noticed that he is almost always aware of the location of the most attractive person, and when a room is too large or contains too many people, the awareness breaks with a feeling like pissing in the sea. After the stadium has drained into the street and part of the crowd annexed and sealed by a train carriage, he is aware for the first time in two hours of someone in particular he is not looking at, and of his own eyes. Reaching my chest my newborn daughter cries more loudly then is overwhelmed by fatigue. She leans everything into my shoulder and turns with her eyes and mouth wide open. She is either hungry or too full. Her experience is never enough or too much. Lying down is vague and watery.

Warm erect touch is explosive and too soon.
Nothing comes into focus. What impresses
on her is a lack, overflowing. Flowing over the
land as well as under it, as memory overlaps
the present, the river also runs away from the
tunnel it disappears into. The transparent
riverbed curves over the buried iris and pupil.
The land does not fit the water. The banks have
burst and silver covers the fields and the bodies.
If I try to imagine what it's like in her mind I
wake from deep sleep to making love only for
it to be finished. I am left with a feeling of alarm
crusted with dry pleasure, while a squirting
dark room bends around a rhythm. I am old
enough to call the imposition a heart and am
reassured by my 'heart' that what I think
just happened did indeed happen to me. I am
anxious that it did: if it were hers, this flooding
love would break her tiny body. The other
father smiles and waves at her in a way that is
not an attempt to communicate with her. I look
in the mirrored wall to see the expression on
my baby's face and see my own face attempting
a photoshoot expression, which turns into the
fake surprise of having to admit to knowing
someone you are hoping not to make eye contact
with, and I am not fooled. The baby has hiccups.
They act severely on her chest, offering her
ribs, which take on the appearance of gills. The
hiccups have the surprising effect of calming.

She seems to be resigned to them, the way
the struggling of a fish in your hand will give
way to an occasional pulse of contrition or
resistance or dying. She is a vehicle for something else's movement: nostalgia. That morning
before she left the house—for the first time
without her mother—she was fed. The breast is
a warm round part of her body that is strangely
removable. Now these hiccups; with each jolt,
the memory of sucking life from a body flows
backwards. Her body is not a safe place to store
milk. Some has pooled on my shoulder. Safety
is corrupted in her stomach: boiled and squirt-
ed downwards. It is odd that intimacy and
embarrassment are the options available for the
fathers to choose from. The mulch smell from
the baby's nappy might have embarrassed the
fathers, but on this occasion they were totally
cool with it. The baby's head began once more
to knock at her father's collarbone. Her father
and mother were always open to their daughter
and yet the baby was always trying madly
to open them. She was already inside; there was
nowhere to go. But she contained something
resistant, hard and unaccountable that neither
love nor law could control or dissolve. It scared
her parents and they were desperate for it not
to disappear. What their daughter knew would
be lost with the ability to express it. It would
be replaced, when she was approved and when

she smiled, by all the wonderful things her parents had been promised, each with a watermarked certificate, rights and obligations. The floor of the lift rises through the fathers' feet as it comes to a stop at the level where they entered. A mobility frame rolls in with a glamorous old woman. She presses the button for the ground floor, composes herself in a corner of the lift and holds out her basket of fudge and stockings for a father to take. She says, That baby is cold. The father wraps his salty baby more tightly in its blanket. The baby is turned and slips into the crook of his arm with its legs tight against his chest. The woman peels back the blanket and runs her eyes over the baby's eye. There is an unprecedented mixing and spread of juices with and around a newborn. You know what it's like, when you want to place your offspring's head entirely in your mouth. The old lady's mouth has a slight quiver. It is very wet and flat. She wears white and orange powders, an Elizabethan look which makes the yellow nicotine patch on her forearm seem like something from the future. Juices such as the baby sick on the chest, the spit left by kisses on the grazes the baby's fingernails cut into her cheeks, the baby's piss between the electric piano keys, the bubbles which form between the baby's lips, popped by the powdered nose of an old woman. I imagine the outline of a dressing table in years of orange powder spilled on stiff brown carpet. The baby in the pram rustles and the woman turns towards it. To move closer to one baby would mean moving further from another. The lift begins to slow. My baby's eyes close. Imagine dark that is busier than light. The warmth between her legs is dissipating and getting louder. She is different from vertical, she senses, and different from hiccups but not different from the heartbeat she is curled around. Her own heartbeat flows inside the slower rhythm. Two rivers run the same channel. You are happy now, the woman says, repeating what the father had said a moment before to his daughter. He had not been sure the words had been spoken. In the old woman's mouth, the sentence was more command than description. If the baby was told it was happy in the present it would in the future become happy. You want everyone in this lift to know that your baby is happy, so they will approve, the woman seemed to be saying when she repeated the father's sentence. The three adults looked at the baby which was supposed to be happy. It was undeniably true, as far as they could tell: she was happy. The twitching behind closed eyelids only accentuated the stillness of the rest of her trusting body. The father replied on behalf of his child, She is. This outing to the shop on his own felt like a test of

what presence he could provide for the child
and what absence he could provide for his wife,
in relieving her of the child for a short part of
the tiring day. He was aware that he was not in
this moment a good judge of the true signifi-
cance of this affirmation of his child's happiness,
as it seemed to him more vital than anything
he had ever previously heard said in relation to
himself or anyone else who had ever existed.
She is: he took care to sound neither triumphant
nor defensive. The woman laughed warmly.
She is, she said. The baby's existence was
no longer in doubt. The father's legs tingled as
a result of the maternal stranger's approval, or
of the smooth movement of the lift. He was
vividly aware of where her feet were in relation
to his. The air in the lift was stale. Some pres-
surised air was released somewhere as the lift
landed. I would have had many babies, the
antique woman said, but I was never a citizen
of this country. By the time I was legal I was old.
She had retrieved her basket of fudge and
stockings and rolled through the doors before
I realised they were open.

My daughter's eyes emerged, wet pigeon replaced by amber. We missed the sweet burnt smell of her drying umbilical nub. She grew fine black hair from the middle of her head and we missed her bald, senile vibe. Her gaze steadied.

We removed her hat and dreams moved across her face and escaped through the top of her head. My beard hairs claimed her cheeks. Her lips kissed ghosts, then began to sync with sounds: zombie words. We supplied the words, day and night, as though she required translation.

My wife and I shared a story about our daughter which began not with conception but with a birth we considered to be good: it was fourteen minutes (or five pages) between us entering the hospital and her entering the world. That story was packed away, stored for future use.

The public myth began when she was named. We returned home from the rite that was not a rite, left the front door on the latch and called it domesticity. Extended family passed through low-lit rooms, narrating how our daughter had grown and who she looked like and where she had come from—uncle or aunt, Devon or the Gulf of Finland. When they left, we tried out her name again in private, still loose on her body.

I thought I had known where I came from but now I wasn't so sure. For ten years, between eight and eighteen, every Monday I travelled back and forth between my father's house and the house where my mother and stepfather live together. My fathers share the same Christian name and both became granddad. It was strange to me that I was my daughter's only father: surely half of what she needs. I needed to find a way of fathering in the singular.

In the cool shower water pooled between my daughter's stomach and mine. I stared at a clock-face on the side of an adjacent building. The clock was always wrong—but always in a refreshing new way. I was convinced, every day, in a refreshing new way, to give myself up to that random clock. Some days lasted twenty-seven hours—why not—and some days barely sputtered into life. Have you ever, during coitus with someone you love, suddenly startled: I have absolutely no idea who you are!? Waking was something like that, every day, several times a day. Mornings
     were
manifestoes. Painting
     red nails
to show how we work in our hiding
     [come back]
places. Beginning by looking back
     to a beginning

by spending a week of convalescence
    peeling an orange
wrapped in the tribe's felt and fat
    after the crash.
Beginning each morning with the future
    fathers are explained
by the Tartar's felt hat,
    the satsuma. Meanwhile
my coming-of-age hides
    in the shoe cupboard. I visit
and find it outraged, refusing to account
    for these new days. The duck's face
when the model speedboat donuts. I convince
    myself to love
even though I do. I forget why I
    entered the cupboard
and the future draws strength from the doubt.
    Today she smiled,
organising mist into a stream. The next day
    we swam and the next day

By the time we dried off it was winter. Our lives became plain and possible. We were seized with the practicalities of moving house. We looked in earnest at newbuild semi-rural semis. I began driving lessons, filled with intense nostalgia for the present with every stall.

In the cooler, more rational air, I could see two models—the revolution never happened —of fatherhood: take over the kitchen or disappear into work. At the library I saw fathers perform one role or the other: intimate but brittle exuberance or benevolent but distant strength. I could see no future in either. Neither seemed true to the lingering startle:

I have absolutely no idea who you are!

Six months after birth, I found that I had developed an alternative set of ambitions as a father:

1 not to betray that uncertainty;
2 to be gentle;
3 to wear matching socks.

My adult male body was large and hard and milkless. My strategy was to make up for biological lack with tools and enthusiasm. I went to a dark green camping shop and bought myself a vest with useful pockets. I strapped my own baby to my chest and ventured out, walking in long circular thoughts, clinking with official equipment.

In cafés I read pages from Russian novels and recent fathering manuals and concluded that I was, in some important respect, the first father who had ever lived.

Out in the snow I dared judgemental old ladies with my eyes to accept that fact. A woman was concerned my baby should be wearing a hat; I produced from one of my many useful pockets a hat, and shouted that it was she, the middle-aged woman, who should be wearing it—to keep her hair on!

I averted my eyes from other young fathers, who seemed to me preposterous.

When I saw friends it was to introduce them to the baby and to say goodbye. We would be leaving the capital soon. They expressed their own longing to breathe cleaner air and mustered serious comments about schools.

I reacted badly, the way I had done a few years before when the same friends bought houses. Our move was, I said, about other things.

My wife and I convened hazardous meetings where life was brokered. We began to ask for a new kind of time that existed outside the household economy: to ourselves. We attempted to give the baby time to itself and it declined the offer. I watched clocks and eyelids and my own voice, which seemed to be taking on a life of its own.

I noticed my wife making plans for future solvency—using her time to herself for things other than other things—and it seemed a feat of prodigious imagination. Instead, I worked on a novel in tensely passionate bursts, reading it to the baby until I could no longer ignore her side of the dialogue:

rapid blink
toe flex
rising sound
falling sound
falling over (from horizontal position)
neck grasp
fingernail moult

It was work without a goal, I told myself; the reward was the labour. When I was there, she needed me. But it made her dependence easier to bear for me to think that I was replaceable. I took comfort in sealing her nappies and sending them out on their journeys, by refuse truck, beyond the known world. If there were parts of my baby scattered everywhere, she would never die.

/

In truth, the best parts of the day were often spent on the sofa. I was a man with a mild codeine habit, happiest being crawled on while watching TV.

Mid-afternoon, there was an advert that made my daughter laugh. A building society had paid poets to sell the company's services. The poets spoke to camera with tears in their eyes. They said that sometimes parents must be prudent as well as wise.

I knew that the baby had made me easy to impress: I was moved by cashiers' interest in my wellbeing and frightened buskers with my applause. Nevertheless I had the feeling that the adverts were speaking directly to me.

I was disappointed the mortgage adviser was not a poet. But once I explained that I was married to someone with prospects, she was pleased to see me.

We provided the necessary PDFs—proof of our wealth, our citizenship—with the same pride that our daughter would, in a few months, display when bringing us her brimming potty.

Once we were awarded the mortgage, the adviser became friendly and asked me what I was writing. I was supposed to be writing a novel, I said, but had lately been devoting my non-fathering time to research about the Russian ancestors from which the money for the house deposit had come.

Eleasar Clases
    Leopold Clases
        Denis Klaces
            Joanna Klaces
                Caleb Klaces
                    Gina Klaces

The person who most interested me in my research was Leopold Clases, my mother's paternal grandfather. I first wrote about Leopold and his father Eleasar in an essay about my parents' divorce—an essay which I forwarded to our mortgage adviser. My father's family are from the East End and my mother's family are Russian and Northern Irish. I was mostly concerned with my Russian ancestors, whose name I inherited, but in the essay I wanted to balance the two sides, in the spirit of the break-up. I reached Leopold by way of my father's former job as an Anglican priest:

Glancing at the indistinct black-and-white photograph of a man in full robe with a long white beard, which has hung for years in my mother's house, I have often tricked myself into seeing what I have never seen elsewhere: my father conducting a sermon. The man is actually Rabbi Wasebo, from my mother's side of the family. He is posing, it's said, in the Tsar's Summer Palace outside St Petersburg, in the year that Dostoevsky was stretched out on his deathbed in the same city, with Anya Grigor'yevna reading to him from the Gospels. Rabbi Wasebo's brother-in-law Eleasar Clases was a Kapellmeister—an orchestral conductor—who lived with his family in the Summer Palace, where his son Leopold, my mother's grandfather, remembered tasting ice cream for the first time and complaining because it was cold. At the turn of the century, when Leopold was six, the family emigrated. They left in such a hurry that Leopold fell from the sleigh and it was some time before the family noticed and went back to fetch him from the snow.

Settled in Denmark, life for the once splendid Jewish family was desperate. Eleasar, ex-Kapellmeister, travelled to Germany in search of work. When he couldn't find any employment, he shot himself.

His son also left Denmark. The Britain Leopold came to in 1912, aged sixteen, did not ask for proof of birth or nationality at its borders. After the war the rules changed: without documentation he could never return home.

Leopold worked in a hotel kitchen, a socialist margarine factory and for the soap-makers Lever Brothers, where he was an accountant. He turned down the offer to live in Port Sunlight, the company's model village near Liverpool. He didn't want to rent. He wanted to own a piece of England.

During the Second World War he joined
the voluntary services and had to present himself
at a police station every week, because he had no
birth certificate to speak on his behalf. His chil-
dren went to a convent school and believed their
father was Danish.

In the first nine months of my daughter's life
I felt I was new to the country. It was a feeling
too precious to share, too claustrophobic to
keep secret. I went directly to Leopold.

I wrote a letter in which my great-grandfather told me, among other things, that his
grave had been dug up and his body exhumed
and reburied a few miles to the west, closer to
the Irish Sea. This was exciting for Leopold,
and relevant to me, because a housing development was being built on the deconsecrated land
where he was formerly interred. He wrote that
as far as he could tell, the houses were going to
be warm, modern, relatively reasonably priced,
English: a perfect place for a young family to
set down roots.

My wife, my daughter and I toured the
show home with a sales representative, Terry,
who told us it was amazing how it was only
three years since he had left Abuja, and already
he owned his own house in Greasby. He had a
way of sweeping his open hand through the
generous space and then of bringing it tightly

into a fist of ownership which I found pro-
foundly affecting.

We watched a groaning JCB through the
show home's window. I've never seen such clear
glass, I said. That's because there's no glass in
there, Terry said. I stretched out my arm to
put my hand through the empty frame and my
fingers were shunted into my hand by glass.
Terry laughed and laughed, until he was cough-
ing and had to suck on an inhaler.

He sat with a cappuccino in a plastic cup
and tried to calm down. Every time he stood he
split into giggles and had to sit again. I looked
out the window—embarrassed, but also there
was a phrase just out of reach. It was about
a JCB doing exactly what this JCB was doing:
slowly inverting the way the earth was ordered,
making a mound of sacred rubbish, which
made it sound as though the activity should
be taken as a metaphor for life, but which also
made clear that I was not naive enough to
believe there can be metaphors for the whole
of life.

I thought about the future Alhambras
built with bricks formed of thousands of layers
of compressed nappies. I thought about my
daughter's children one day working in skyscrapers constructed from plastic toy sediment.

Your daughter, Terry said. The show home
has a wall missing.

/

The theme of National Poetry Day was 'Light'.
A literary organisation commissioned poets to
write on the subject in relation to particular times
of day, hoping to create a collaborative poem
which could be read non-stop for twenty-four
hours. I was assigned 2 a.m.

I used the money to go on holiday to a Scottish
island with my wife and daughter: a bridge
between our old life in the capital and our new
life on Leopold's grave.

It was the first time my daughter had been
on holiday. I didn't want to describe my life
with her as though it was a poem. In fact, I
wanted to write myself away from her, to begin
to set some territory apart.

But together we had an intense experience
at 2 a.m. National Poetry Day was in a week.
I decided the poem had something to contribute
to the memory.

When I look up
at this time
of night
wherever I am
is always only
almost where it is.
Another, better, more
expansive canopy

lies just beyond
what I can make out:
darker sky and whiter stars and
altogether more depth, clarity, purity,
a more stylish, ancient, sparse, deep night
of which the limited
dome I can see
is just one pale
and diffident
part.
To venture towards the inaccessible
I had a baby
and bought a car.
I didn't know how to
turn off the headlights
nor be persuaded
a baby
cannot turn off.
An intense perverse
horizontal light
struck across the remote island
which weighed a dark vertical
stack of space
onto the car.
My daughter was
exhausted, finally asleep
and misshapen by
her attempts to
sleep.
Electric light crawled

the car's interior edge
fading towards
the middle
where the baby's routine cry
was all she took with her.
She is not present
for her own
accusation.
I drove along the lane
to a farm
and there performed a three-point
turn and remembered
my driving instructor.
I would have liked
to hear him whistle
with joy
at the unbelievable
incompetence
one last time.
It was always
so romantic
when the streetlights
came on
and he pretended
not to notice,
I wonder
how he would brush off the advance
of two-thirty
in the morning. The route
from home back to

home. The experience
which is
already the commentary
on the experience.
He said,
Thinking is the enemy
of driving.
In the same way
look how
this night
has been transformed
by the hardship
in the back seat
into a
more authentic,
more deep and necessary
experience for you
than all your previous
attempts
to take in the night,
which have been ruined by too much thought,
which was the revelation I had been looking for.
The car
and its headlights, however,
have rolled forward
in advance of your
advance
to have met the hedge
where headlights
and moonlight

crash. Late cold pedals
on bare feet. The second thing you think is
how busy it is in the hedge. No engine
there was the sound
of rain
but it was moths
on the bonnet. I beat my heart
and watched
my daughter's eyelids.
The lights broken so
inside and outside
passed freely.
The hour, three-eleven
in the morning,
had finally made its way
down to the car
and a pair of cow's eyes appeared through
the hedge
and I was devastated
the baby
was sleeping through
the profound experience
of the island night
and impatient
and alone so
leant into the back
and
the regret
developing
in the mouth

with the unbelievable
incompetence
as her eyes
opened black, wild and frightened
but there was no sound. She was awake
but for the first time in her life
no sound. From my mouth
as if it was an awkward situation
a commentary
explaining to her
about this time of night, how
when I look up
at this time
of night
wherever I am
is always only
almost where it is, how
another, better, more
expansive canopy
lies just beyond
what I can make out, and how
on this island with you
as my driving instructor
noted
everything seemed altogether different
until you woke.

/

In the pile of holiday post on the doormat was a letter from Terry, the asthmatic sales representative. He had crossed out the company letterhead and written *PERSONAL*. He complimented us on our daughter, who was a very fast crawler, and on our taste in houses. He said that there was something he needed to say, he was sorry to say, which was that he saw us in our car afterwards.

We loved everything about our new house, or about the house that would be ours when it was built. The structure was solid and optimistic. It occupied a boundary between two areas, one old and rich, the other new and deprived. A gentle river described the edge of the development. You could see the stars over the fields. Most important of all, it was where my great-grandfather had been buried.

A show home, we learnt from our visit, must be approachable and warm, and not too personalised. The framed photographs on the mantelpiece were of relatively happy, unmemorable faces. The *Encyclopedia Britannica* on the bookshelves went up to 'P'. I wondered, after we had frantically run up the stairs and saved our daughter from the open wall, whether the developer had purposefully left the show home unfinished. It gave the imagination somewhere to go.

The effect of this ordinary, hard-working interior decoration, and incompletion, and of the relief that our daughter was alive, and of the decision to get into huge debt, was to arouse me and my wife. Often this is what arousal feels like to me: a compulsion to complete what I otherwise can't complete; to pay back debts I can't pay back. Our daughter had fallen asleep in the car. A row of yew trees blocked the view between the road and the site of the new development. The small church was locked. We proceeded as if no one was looking.

Over several evenings, we composed a reply to Terry. My wife interpreted Terry's letter as saying little more than what it said: if we were in the habit of having sex in our car he wanted to warn us to be more discreet. I suspected his letter was the beginning of a blackmail.

The main pleasure of sex in the car was the shared fantasy about what we were doing. The sex itself was a distant point of physical intensity buried under a great many frames of reference. There were all the unforgiving contours of the car, then there were our bodies, which were mostly covered and even more inaccessible than usual, and there was the complicated pressure of the moment, and of the presence of the baby asleep in the back, and of the unfinished fear that she could have fallen through an unbuilt wall. The car was densely packed with our new responsibilities. The sex seemed to need all the variously

entangled pressures to push against but did
not push them away; the sense of responsibility
and the sex intensified one another.

We thanked Terry for the tip-off; then said
we were embarrassed but not regretful or
ashamed; then we emphasised how much the
house meant to us, because it was where my
great-grandfather Leopold Clases' bones were
buried. We debated what to say about Leopold.
At first, we wrote that he was the son of a great
military musician. We talked about pogroms,
The Pale and suicide. Then we decided that
sounded too grand. Instead, we wrote about
Leopold's life in England. He was just a child
when he arrived. He soon fell in love with
an English woman, a waitress whose father was
a gardener at Lincoln Cathedral. It was only
through relentless hard work that he ended up
owning his own house.

Whilst we were writing the letter our daughter was teething, restless and uncomfortable.
One afternoon, when I fetched her from her nap
and placed her on the carpet with her toys,
she turned away from me and towards the floor
and let out a slow rising cry like a goose. For
the first time in her life, it occurred to me there
might be no somatic or environmental reason
for this cry. She might just be sad. This affected
me in a surprising way. It brought me despair,
obviously, but I was also relieved—because for

once it wasn't a procedural issue, and in procedural issues such as an empty stomach or a full nappy, she and I were rarely equals. The sadness brought us closer because all I could do was understand.

It also made me rethink the whole letter to Terry. It should focus on how important it was for our daughter to grow up somewhere happy and safe and meaningful. This had little to do with the subject of Terry's letter. But it sounded persuasive to us. We introduced a line about it fulfilling our dream of solid walls and a strong garden fence. We weren't sure why the fence was suddenly important, we just knew it was.

While we were reworking our letter to emphasise to Terry his central role in our daughter's life, another letter arrived. This time the letterhead was not crossed out. In this official letter, Terry, the enthralling but also pragmatic housing expert, said the developer required greater assurance of our ongoing financial strength. He said the checks were routine but obligatory.

I wrote straight back, against my wife's advice and wishes, with an aggressive portrait of Leopold. I told Terry I was speaking to him as a person and as a father, not as a homebuyer. I believed I could appeal to the vulnerable asthmatic in him. I let him into the truth: my ongoing financial security, and therefore

my ability to buy this house, was contingent
on my ability to write, and my ability to write
depended on living in this particular house,
because this house, above all other houses, was
meaningful to me and my young family, as
it was deeply, tangibly connected to my recent
ancestor, my model ancestor who had, like all of
us, worked extremely hard and been extremely
frugal and honest and finally bought himself a
home and set up his children for life.

As a recent immigrant yourself, I added,
I suspect you sometimes worry that your children may lose contact with that part of you
which is part of somewhere else—let alone
your children's children, and your children's
children's children. Since leaving Russia, every
generation of my family has moved; every
child has settled somewhere new. Leopold has
continued to travel even after his death.
Perhaps his bones, like you, will always be
one step ahead of us.

The point is that Leopold Clases, Terry's
short reply stated, sadly has not been one of the
bodies exhumed on the site of the future estate.

Then the story
collapsed.

The engine cut out and the boat enjoyed the
water.

On the street
first the baby's hands then the feet curling
a ripple from the hands to the feet
back to the hands because:
DOG.
The finger moves towards the dog before
bouncing off.

The floor rises to the collapse,
offering me a short form to fill in.
If only someone really was asking me a few
quick questions in order to fill in a short form
that would be great.

Desire goes up one more floor than exist,
where it sighs open
and there is a dog. Dog. Dog. Dog. Dog. It's a
dog isn't it. Dog. Dog. Dog.
    Dog. Dog. Dog. Dog. Dog. It's a dog.
Dog
Let's look at something
Dog
How would you identify the body?
Dog
Dog

Dog

I heard scuffling upstairs. A baby was trapped in the baby's bedroom.

Its wings, good for flight, were too big for it. They hit the window and sent the baby backwards. Its forked tail, beautiful in flight, flicked waste across the sill.

I jumped every time it flapped. With each jump I became more convinced that I did not want to see the baby compromised like this.

I spoke to the baby. I told it 'we' were going to get it out. (Me and the other adults? Me and the person speaking? Me and it? Me and its beauty?)

Eventually we got my hands around it.

Dignity was restored. It felt exactly, beautifully, as I imagined it: a space where the baby would be.

I heard scuffling upstairs. A space where the baby would be was trapped in the baby's bedroom.

Its wings, good for flight, were too big for it. They hit the window and sent the space where the baby would be backwards. Its forked tail, beautiful in flight, flicked waste across the sill.

I jumped every time it flapped. With each jump I became more convinced that I did not want to see the space where the baby would be compromised like this.

I spoke to the space where the baby would be. I told it 'we' were going to get it out. (Me and the other adults? Me and the person speaking? Me and it? Me and its beauty?)

Eventually we got my hands around it.

Dignity was restored. It felt exactly, beautifully, as I imagined it: a swallow.

I heard scuffling
    Keep your hands where I can see them
    and step away/from the image

Downstairs, my wife closed her laptop and took the baby from me.

/

Terry was the first person to visit us in our new house. He brought flowers for us and a hat for our daughter, which he said he had picked up scoping out real estate in Vietnam. He made us promise to set up our writing desks as a first priority. He joked that he found our style very persuasive.

Our new house was haunted by the scratching of sharp feet and the deluxe bass of strong wings. The sight of the swallows above the cool evenings filled me with relief. They looked like freedom, and they were real.

We watched them leave for South Africa

without knowing they were leaving. The next day it began to rain.

Our daughter now had her own bedroom and bedtime. We worked to a routine, complete with transition rituals.

After writing for three hours each day, I placed my laptop and notebooks in a drawer just out of reach of my daughter's hands, which tested every handle they could find.

After putting our daughter to bed in the evening, my wife and I lay on the floor next to an electric fire and drank cups of rooibos and listened to what we imagined was rain falling on the wings of migrating swallows.

If we were able to get up again, we crossed our legs on the floor and wrote descriptions of designer sunglasses from a brighter season: Spring/Summer collection. In this way we would pay for furniture.

My wife and I finished each other's sentences. Then rewrote them. The skill is to sound the opposite of how most parents want to sound: as though something is at stake, when nothing is at stake. We were good at producing vague status anxiety, in order to dissolve it with the meaningless authority of the brand.

These were tender and precious working evenings. For my wife it was labour in addition to a new full-time job, which itself was on top of part-time childcare. I felt I was making some headway with my novel, although the more time my daughter and I spent apart, the more fathers and daughters appeared in my fiction. Both my wife and I were grateful for something which required the other to be present, sharing other-than-care.

This evening we had started with shades and moved on to reading poems, managing to say them out loud if we put on voices, but seeking reassurance, sincerely, that there can be room in language for thought. And what would Samuel Taylor Coleridge have done had the subject of his description woken up and screamed?

Upstairs, I laid my daughter back down to sleep. I patted her lightly on the back. She stood up. I placed her down again and patted her again, more firmly. She stood up, arguing blindly in half-formed words. I braced my body ready to push her down again.

My wife appeared and suggested a walk. We had written all that was required that evening; there was a rare lift in the constant rain. I washed my hands—this had become a habit, an alternative—and hugged my wife.

We talked into the air, easing from the puzzle-logic mind of copywriting into something looser, more in tune with the baby. That was it: the baby was beginning to agree with some of our adult terms. She and we all knew,

for example, where we could find her *feet*.
But she would also shout *feet!* at the stars above
our house. Her naming was not yet to solve
the problem of the world. Her words and our
thoughts slid about with the swans on the river
in the dark.

The Angler was conspicuous in his camouflage. We nodded a greeting as though we had
greeted before. I noticed a baby monitor beside
his tub of worms. I wanted to tell him I found
his nonchalance inspirational.

He introduced himself as Andrew. He asked
us how we were settling in and said that since
the two of them had moved out to the estate, his
daughter had slept like a log.

He was older than us, in his later thirties
I guessed. He was softly spoken, giggly and too
direct. I suspected his aura of chill was pharma-
ceutically aided.

We asked him what he was fishing for.
He ignored the question and explained that the
parts of the estate that looked wildest to me
—the dreamy, rough meadow-type areas—were
in fact planted by the developer. They were the
parts of the land where the factories had stored
their waste before it leaked into the river. He
said that the developer had underestimated the
capacity of the meadows, should the river burst
its banks, and built the houses too close. He
said he was starting a community action group

63

to lobby for better flood defences.

I nudged my wife and agreed that we had to keep the baby moving. My preferred distraction from work was reading about extreme weather events in countries where I had never been. There was not enough room in my head for streams as well as tsunamis. What interested me was that there had been a factory here, not a graveyard. The river had been red. Humans clean up human mess with meadows. Fathers plant themselves where they imagine their forefathers to have been.

The first sips of a pint had never tasted so good. By the third sip I was drunk. My wife and I held hands over the table and congratulated one another for everything.

Returning from the bar with two whisky chasers, I found Andrew at the table with my wife. They had just arranged, they said, for me and Andrew and our daughters to meet up and go to a gallery. Do some fathering together.

As long as I don't have to join your flood group, I said.

/

After the long period when I lived by the random clock, I realised that not only did I have to buy clothes before our daughter grew out of them,

I had to decide whether they were blue or pink. She had entered the world of symbols.

When we went to purchase our symbol—the one we decided our daughter needed to feel at home in her new home—the young man at the pet shop advised that two hamsters are better than one. He said that he himself had twenty-three hamsters—which made two seem like barely any hamsters.

My hamsters love me, he said.

I believed him.

I soon needed our hamsters to love me. I liked cleaning their cage with my daughter and sending the shit-sawdust out across the oceans. I liked, I admit, when my daughter misjudged the firmness of her grip, to which I could be unambiguous:

That is wrong. You can see, can you not, that the animal is in pain?

Because I am the kind of urban, abstract environmentalist who cannot judge when a river is likely to flood my garden and who doesn't have moral rules about animals' pain. I was jealous, in fact, of my daughter's easy connection with the non-human.

But *thou*, my babe! shalt wander like a breeze
By lakes and sandy shores, beneath the crags
Of ancient mountain, and beneath the
   clouds—

Coleridge's son Hartley is so extremely quiet
it makes the poet think in strange ways. 'Frost
at Midnight' is an escapist poem that I found
useful. I had been shaken by my capacity,
during the night, for force. I needed the poem to
help me keep striving for its sheer gentleness.

But the poem might be *too* useful. The
baby does nothing at all, except breathe. Its
breath fills the gaps between the father's
strange thoughts.

And as if that wasn't quiet enough, young
Hartley then becomes the *breeze*. The father
mistakes his son for his own words, then for
the weather.

In the morning we found one hamster
tattered in sticky blood, while the other looped
the tunnels in vigilant mania. I could not
articulate how, precisely, this disturbed my
daughter's thoughts and my own, but I knew
we had to disturb them back to normal.

The young man at the pet shop said that
peculiar hamster behaviour is almost always
attributable to an unstable and/or violent
human environment.

This one you sold us doesn't work properly,
I said. Please provide a replacement.

I tried to explain to Andrew why I wanted words to stay away from my child, regardless of how she abused them and the fact that they were mostly Dog.

I was driving the four of us to an exhibition. I had seen Andrew a few times in the evening down by the river and had warmed to his vacant enthusiasm, but there was no easy exit from this conversation and I was nervous.

I told him that my daughter has the rest of her life to be mediated. It seemed too soon for language to come and remove the world in order for us to share it.

Andrew told me not to be afraid of what my daughter will say about me. He said it was language that meant his own daughter slept so astonishingly well,

Isn't it darling?

In the mirror I looked at the pale, stern girl sat next to my daughter. My daughter gave each new sight one of her small collection of sounds. Andrew's daughter spoke when she was spoken to and responded in a low voice,

Indeed.

Indeed, Andrew repeated. Language does indeed ease separation, he said. When you leave the room, the kid has words to keep it company.

Neither child was interested in the colourful sculptures. My daughter blew raspberries on the glass door, turned, took one look at the art, lay down and sobbed into the polished concrete.

This time, she did not seem sad or scared. She seemed to be saying that I had brought her all this way to trap her in an empty room. The plump organic forms are compelling to adults because they're erotic and distantly familiar: this is how looking felt when we were babies. But to a baby, they're so familiar as to be almost invisible.

I suggested this to Andrew, in halting sentences, while I tried to piece my daughter back together in my arms. By way of an answer, Andrew asked his daughter if she liked the sculptures.

Before she could reply I tossed my keys on the floor. As I'd hoped, Andrew's daughter strode over to pick them up. The invigilator moved his copy of *Regarding the Pain of Others* even closer to his spectacles. Andrew giggled uneasily. An older couple left the room. I darted between the sculptures jangling the keys. Laughter sputtered through the children. They were crazy for the keys. They walked their wide-legged walks as quickly as they could while they squealed. I ran into a corner and dropped the keys behind me, nonchalant. They ran in zig-zags and disappeared into the corner, where I could not see them. Then a cry.

Indeed! Andrew's daughter moaned and moaned. Indeed! she wailed.

Andrew picked her up and curved his body around her. He carried her out of the room without a glance back.

My own daughter appeared. She held the keys in the air but both of us knew her triumph was hollow.

/

Andrew was sure that he and his daughter were fine to take the bus. They needed to take a moment, regroup.

Buying my daughter a meal in a café was, during that time, one of my greatest pleasures. I liked the neatness of it, and the way the two of us were more demonstrably equal than at other times, and I liked the way it gave the impression I was financially comfortable.

But that day, after Andrew had indeed left, wounded, our burritos did not taste chillicious. However annoying I found Andrew and his zoned-out affection, I needed to know if my daughter had hurt his daughter.

She said nothing. She uncurled curly fries. She said Worm.

I gave up. I wrote the exchange down on my phone because there was no one to say it to, even though she was sitting in front of me.†

Now I needed language. When we got home I looked around our new front room and *named*. If she knew the names of things then she could tell me what she had done.

Looking around, my possessions confused me: half belonged to a random teenager, half belonged to an old man. Only one item mattered to my daughter. Hat. The present from Terry. Hat was massive and decorated with a bright woollen bird spreading its wings for flight. In her new bedroom, she slept in Hat.

I sensed that, despite the sobs, she was relieved when I finally left her alone lidded with her new totem in her new bedroom—relieved not to have to cling to me. Her attachment had become painful to her. When I closed the bedroom door behind me I was,

Daddy come back. Put Hat on. No, no, no.

/

The summer was over. I was teaching one module at a university and volunteering as a weather data collector: research for my novel. Lesson plans and methane emissions spread out across the bed. The day placed demands on the night.

Despite my efforts, language seemed to provide my daughter no comfort. The nights were blisteringly strange, burning up the thin veil of familiarity beginning to spread across the spoken world. Waking at the point of falling asleep, again and again, holding a small, wild body that rose and kept rising against my stubbornness, which was desperately sovereign.

Sometimes, it was like trying to pull my heart out of my chest/sometimes cruelty is easy.

Either way, mornings broke like promises. We reminded ourselves of our reasons: not just to sleep but to give the parents some portion of the day in which they might be quietly intimate.

To me this meant sex. The intensity of the thing when it happened shocked both of us. Were we using one another to escape from the family that our sex had made? From behind a closed door a small, hoarse voice said,

No, no, no.

/

As soon as she woke, before sunrise, I took her out to explore our new surroundings by bike.

The air was pink and grey and the scenery was unresolved. From her seat in front of me, over the handlebars, the infant spoke into the wind. I replied into the wind. Together we constructed what we saw, and lost our words to what we constructed.

We named the roads of the new development. We named the river that divided the development. We named the snot on our faces and the wet leaves that stuck in her seat. In my daughter's grammar the scenery was full of strange purpose. Nouns were also verbs. Effects led to causes. The stage speaks on the actors' behalf. The animals have feelings. The landscape paints the characters and rolls the river up into a lake, which is here

to support the falling light.

The pale blue pleasure-boat is here to slip towards the small horizon.

The inflatable vodka luge is here for happy hour.

The infant is here to learn to appreciate landscapes.

The dog is here to chew the surface of the lake.

The factory supplies the lake with a pink streak of chemical effluent, here to provide local jobs and use up the father's pot of cadmium red.

The boat's wake is here to reconcile the chemical pink with the reflected auburn flare of late sunlight.

The young teacher walks through loosened light to relieve himself of the day.

The patient runs towards him, away from the holy water.

The off-duty ship mechanic is below deck to criticise the barman's pouring angle.

The electric light below deck is increasingly soulful.

The captain is here to imagine ways the sunset could sour.

The use of multiple vanishing points: the effect it might have on passengers.

Points vanish into waves and waves into points because the father is familiar with the photon.

The amateur photographer is here to avoid introspection.

The retired triathlete is here to rescue the three-legged dog from polluted water.

The inflatable luge is here to rescue the retired triathlete.

The infant's ice cream is here to melt into the eczema on the wet dog's muzzle.

The stag party is here because who else will sing in praise of the sunset.

The climber has stepped off the mountains in fear not of darkness but its onset.

The infant is here to appreciate everything her mother has given up.

The mountains rise up to resist the Earth's turn.

High in the futile mountains, the purpose of the suddenly dense grey cloud is unclear, nor is the father sure he is responsible.

The actors are here to popularise the bar. Time is marked by the fading of the actors' talent.

Shafts of light broach the subject of the lake with the father.

Passengers scramble for the heat of returning care.

The new, weak care has no width or height.

A thin covering of heavier care helps reconcile the boat's movement with its mass.

The beard hairs stuck in the foreground pines are here to show the father's long-sightedness.

The new, weak, stiff, yellow care is here to remind the teacher of the armpits of his cheap shirt.

The cheap shirt is here to expose the working conditions inside the factory.

At last, the father leaves the sunlight alone.

On the cobbles the prostitute wobbles to prove the sun has gone down.

The streetlights are lit to show who lights the streetlights.

The scene is flung upwards and comes down greyscale.

Grainy shadows bring depth to the patient's restrained body.

The doctor imagines the patient's great effort not to be aroused by her own body.

The long blonde hairs from the father's head, curling in the pine trees, are here to remind him he is also inside the scene.

The body gets everywhere.

The infant rearranges the words to make a different father.

Uh-oh.

The back tyre was flat. The rim bumped on the gravel. We were several miles from home, in an empty park.

Uh-oh, she said. Uh-oh. Uh-oh—dissolving into laugh.

I got off the bike and kissed her cheek.

Fok!

I did not correct her.

A woman pulled up. She asked if she could help.
I said no.

She laughed an improbably good-looking laugh.
She lay her bike in the grass and got out a
puncture repair kit. She said she was surprised
I didn't have one in one of my many pockets.

I put my daughter down from the seat.

> You are a good Samaritan, I said.

> I am a Christian but that is not why I am
> helping you, she said.

I turned my wedding ring around my finger.

> She said, How is the river today?

> I said, You know.

But I didn't know. I didn't know how to describe the river, let alone how it might be doing
on any given day. I turned to my daughter and
said,

> How is the river today?

My daughter said that the river was particularly watery today.

Let her speak for herself, said the woman.

Speak for yourself, I said to my daughter.

No, said my daughter.

Are you going to thank me? asked the woman.

On her first birthday I photocopied two letters
from a reproduction of a painted inscription
by the poet and artist David Jones. When David
Jones wrote a letter to tell his mother about a
mustard gas attack from the Ypres front line,
she replied that he spelled like a four-year-old
and should be ashamed of himself. I remembered that story when the tattoo artist, Joshua,
stopped and stared at his unfinished work with
what seemed to be a very pained smile (red
teardrop below left eye). I was convinced that
David Jones and I had managed to misspell
the initials of my wife and my daughter. Joshua
surprised me. He had decided, he said, not to
charge me for his work. Because of karma. It is
good for me to give you this, Joshua said. Pass
it on. *Pass it on*, he repeated. I started to cry.
Joshua changed the subject. He asked me how
pink I would like the pink square between
the two letters, copied from the original paint.
We agreed on the most innocent bubblegum
pink—which he told me the ink brand called
'Fifth Dimension: Nebula'. We joked about when
I would come back to add more letters. I didn't
know that my wife was pregnant, nor that we
would lose the baby. I didn't know that the pink
square was for the

Having written into my arm, and having
written into my arm a memorial as well
as a dedication, I found I was unable to write
anything else, however much time I had in the
day, an inability which felt like someone had
removed my chair. This happened—someone
removed my chair—during circle time at playgroup above a church in the city. It was the
church that the woman who had fixed my puncture attended. The puncture and the constant
rain made playgroup more attractive than
bike rides. The playgroup volunteers tried to
sneak in some Christianity each week. It was
Hallowmas, they told us, and the veil between
the afterlife and the visible world of the elem-
ents was thin. The fancy dress theme was
saints. I dressed my fifteen-month-old daughter in green velvet and white silk, which is
what I imagined was the attire of an affluent
Jewish child in St Petersburg at the turn of the
century. I made my wife late for work insisting
she appreciate the historical accuracy of the
charity shop outfit. She kissed my forehead and
reiterated that she really didn't mind paying
the bills. Then, of course, I handed our daughter
the iPad and offered to take my wife upstairs.
Too soon, replied my wife, stepping out of
the front door. Just enjoy your day and write
while she is asleep. The door closed. Instead of
getting myself a chair, I stood in the middle

of playgroup while everyone sat, and swung my daughter around, showing clearly that I was unaffected by the slight of the removal of the chair. I imagined around me only pale Russian children in green velvet and white silk. I imagined each of these children armed with a small personally engraved knife with which they cut their way through tundra. I imagined that these same indestructible children were also prodigiously sensitive. They were unable to bear the sound of beautiful music. They were spirits who would not break the Duplo or salivate on the plastic animals. There are at least three places around St Petersburg called the Summer Palace. Here are some things the Russian language has to say about Leopold: he had plenty of butter on his head; his appetite came during eating; his elbow is so close, yet he can't bite it! Leopold's son, my maternal grandfather, designed the waste system at the Lever soap factory. What a beautiful labour: keeping a soap factory clean! Anything can become a test. Often it is only my daughter who knows the rules. She pushes me back through doors she must open for me

　　Open for me

　　Open for me

　　Open for me/You cannot pass through the door enough times to enter the room. It is a rule of the playgroup that a parent is not allowed to say that they sleep well. This is especially true for fathers. We say we are tired but are not too tired to dream the playgroup, with its weak squash and sticky chocolate fingers, dry Christian smell, a stage-set constructed from memory. My daughter was dropping a model car down another man's shirt. He explained the weather's recent sulk in terms of school catchment areas. There is an invisible line dividing the city into rain and shine. I did not like this father, who was kind and made me feel unoriginal. He talked about his exciting partner, an academic who studies rave culture. On the weekend, they leave the child with the child's grandparents and go to clubs. It's the same but different, he said. Now he and his partner party to produce data—they wear smart watches and record everything about the experience on special laminated forms. You can get surprisingly good at filling out forms while spangled, he said. This was what it meant to grow up. It was the conversion of a church into a strip-lit MDF box for muted care and leisure. A young Christian mother handed me a free cup of sugary instant coffee. *This is the best cup of coffee I have ever had*, I thought. It occurred to me then that the way I wanted to grow up was to do different things, not the same things I used to do while simultaneously filling out a form. If only I knew what different things were. At that

moment the vicar shuffled in. He was a man
made of something melted. His teacup and
saucer trembled in front of his robes. The vicar
noticed that I did not have a chair and brought
me one. The children, he said, look well.
They began to sing. The vicar sang along and
forgot the words and laughed at his biscuit.
I was ready to follow this man into any battle.

/

I left the pushchair near the cathedral doors
and looked up. The boring old Church of
England, I thought, is where all of advertising's
oversights are hidden. None of this earnest,
chilly, inflexible business have I yet been sold
—and yes, I want it. I want to get out of myself
and fly up to the rafters to seek out a finer dust.
A voice spoke. My daughter looked everywhere
for the man. Where is the man? I pointed, point-
lessly, to the crackling speaker. That is not the
man. How to account for a voice without a body.
How to account for a life lost before it has been
born. The miscarriage left a space where a baby
would be. It was a space that it seemed to me,
then, the building had been built to house
—to stop it from expanding until it swallowed
the world. How many unborn children must
have passed through the cathedral inside their
mothers? A secret hand on and inside the

stomach beneath the dress. How many public hymns were elegies in private? Songs to mark the passing of humans who never grew even to be strangers to their parents. I thought that if anyone could explain that absence to me, could give me a way to respect it and love it without becoming it, it would be someone here—a stranger. Perhaps it would be everyone here, centuries of them, who could disperse me among them as a stranger. Standing to our right was a woman on her own. She looked badly in need of the sustenance of a communion wafer. Newspaper spilled out of the bottom of her tracksuit bottoms. She was mortally high. But she knew every word of the service, of every hymn, without consulting the sheet. I felt the hours of dedicated repetition—she must have had a guardian unselfish and hard enough to make her learn the words. My daughter was walking away from me, towards a face carved into the wall. Between me and her were a mother, father and son all struggling to read, sing and look kindly on us at the same time. I studied them all equally: any one of them might have touched the sacred. Perhaps all of them were blessed. Perhaps to touch the space where the baby would be one must either be ruined or obsessively ordinary. Perhaps that was my choice: go mad or go sane. Perhaps, the priest said through the speaker, we should pause and consider Joseph. Joseph was much more than a child with a towel on his head in a school assembly. Joseph, the priest said, bravely took care of a child not of his own blood. He was a stepfather who trained his stepson Jesus in what he knew how to do, which was carpentry. He lost the child he loved. Unlike God the Father, Joseph the stepfather was not also the Son; Joseph the stepfather was just a man who had risked love for a body that had arrived as a stranger. The son Joseph lost was not Joseph's to give. Yet he loved him and lost him no less. A hand touched me on the shoulder and I jumped. It was a teenager in uniform, motioning for me to follow. I apologised for my baby's inappropriate something. I apologised for my singing too high or too low. The teenager led me in a long, slow walk around the congregation. I carried my daughter, who wanted to show me she had found the speaking man and to walk over and touch his robe. The cathedral employee took us into a side room. It was an ornate chamber of unpainted sandstone, sculpted so as to bring to mind tree roots at the same time as maths. There was an older man in what looked like a rented police outfit, standing over the pushchair, about to detonate.

On All Saints Day, metres replaced months.
A recorded phone message from the Environment Agency told me that the river was at
3.5 metres. Flood risk was purple. A flood action
group leaflet dropped through our door. I
avoided walking on the estate in case I bumped
into Andrew.

My wife was unsure about her planned trip.
It would be the first time she would spend more
than a single night away from the two of us.
She said that if the river was at 3.5 metres and
the flood risk was purple she should stay. Neither
of us really knew what 3.5 metres and purple
meant. We both knew that my wife was more
worried about me.

She had not had any time to herself, even
after the miscarriage. She had taken care of her
daughter, the same as me, and she had also
worked. I wanted her to feel free and I wanted
her to leave so that we could be reunited.

I told her that there was no way that Terry,
the eagle-eyed and generous sales representative,
would have sold us a home on a floodplain. Who
knows—she might even take the rain with her.

I had detailed plans for the week. I had bought
a dozen packets of organic toddler snacks.
I had downloaded vouchers for the aquarium
and packed the dewy swimming bag. I had
checked the Christian calendar for the playgroup
fancy dress.

I had been writing again, with renewed purpose, when our daughter went, a few mornings a week, to nursery—still placing my notebooks and laptop with ceremony in the top drawer when my time was up. If I could use the evenings after she went to bed, I reckoned I could have a draft of the novel by the end of the week.

First I had to do my volunteering. After saying goodbye at the station, I drove my daughter to the fields. I parked outside a pub, walked past the village hardware store, lifted her over the stile and onto my shoulders along the muddy track that hugged the hedgerow.

I boasted about the Unified Model, for which I collected data: the best weather prediction suite in the world. It is based on a map which divides the entire planet into seventeen types of environment. Data from individual points on the map, some fixed and some—such as freighters measuring wind speed—on the move, are extrapolated to make predictions. It takes an entire power plant's energy to run the supercomputers. I told my daughter that when this energy is derived from solar and wind, the weather will power the prediction of itself, in a monstrous closed loop of time past, present and future.

I showed her how I measured the exchange of carbon dioxide, water vapour and energy between the biosphere and atmosphere. I told her about the graphs which showed the steady rise in greenhouse gases and the corresponding rise in temperatures. I told her that there had been more rainfall in the past week than in an average year.

She identified the bright steel frame of the micrometeorological tower as a tree.

/

At the swimming baths, she watched me get changed and chided me for not tying myself in at the waist.

For much of the first year of her life, my intelligence migrated from my head to my body. It was amazing, being so huge, so powerful and so emotionally dependent on the touch of a creature whose mind was mysterious. From when she woke us up to when I closed her bedroom door behind me in the evening, there was something on the tip of my tongue.

All of her fluffy animals, regardless of species and gender, were *Anne*—and I got it. I too felt like a collective. 'Mama' and 'Dada' were omnipotent on one another's behalf. Part of myself was outside myself; responsibility was connection. You were there, remember, you were part of the group?

I watched my daughter fill buckets, spill

secrets. She laughed like a drain.

As she approached her first birthday, outlines emerged. She knew she was different.
When her mother came home from work, she
reacted as to pop music: a dance which rose
and spilled across the boundary of her skin to
become a conscious, fraught offering: a hug.
But adults, like outlines, come and go. She woke
whispering *bye*. She came and went—to nursery—and left me in the world we had shrunk
to the size of a pocket.

In the pool I watched another father, with
a spider tattoo across his forehead, mouth along
to the distorted music: *Like a bird set free...*

She began to walk and talk and slept through
to the morning, and dreaming was confined to
the night. The nights were less risky. My dreams
were no longer short, strange and moving
but long, familiar and horrific. Running after
was impossible to distinguish from running
away. In the daytime I was no longer living the
other life. The domestic turned against me.
It reproached me for what I didn't earn and for
what I hadn't written—for being a father who
needed his daughter's protection.

I did not trust my hands. I scrubbed them so
often they were raw. I steered the car with the
tips of my fingers.

In the back, she sweetened her face with ice
cream. Dada lick Gina lick it, she said. Her most

recent language game was to be a sentence's subject and object both. Carry Gina carry. Her toy pushchair arrived knowing how to put herself inside and push. Teddy bear was put out to bed but as hay hits the head it's morning for Gina. Are you small or far away? Otherwise the bread will starve. Why are you headbutting your fist?

/

On Saturday morning, she climbed into my bed and asked if her mum was in the bin. I asked her if she wanted pancakes. She said that her hamsters would like a lot of strawberries on her pancakes.

Downstairs, I impersonated a storm to make her laugh and banged my head on the corner of the cabinet door.

I lay on the floor very hot. Then I was some-where else.

It was a darkness which welcomed me firmly. I was intensely present but had nothing to do with my body.

I was coiled inside the oily darkness, a story compressed into a premise: I had a decision to make.

My daughter was standing over me. I smiled at her. I waited for the weight to fall through me. The weight did not fall through me.

I thought it was funny that it was not within my power to decide to go back to where I'd been, in order to make the decision, and it was also excruciating.

I wanted to go back.

My daughter laid a blanket over my sweaty chest and said,

Night, night.

She wasn't convinced. She lay down and motioned for me to put her to bed—so the play, at least, was the right way round.

The medics ticked tiny boxes on a huge yellow form. My brief account of what had happened was superseded by data. I didn't understand my heart rate and blood pressure but was happy that my experience was not what had happened to me. My daughter was jealous of the medics' attention. I bragged that I was going to get stitches.

They left and another medic arrived. He had a shaved head and bright blue eyes. He nodded to me then spent a long time laying out a great number of medical items with solemn care. I drank tea and felt genteel, embarrassed and flattered by his dumb performance.

He angled my head into the window's cold light. I moved slowly, enjoying his care. There was a smell of lavender on his body. He was tentative with the scissors so as not to leave a conspicuous hole in my hair. I felt a needle prick my head and three metallic shifts of juice. Then a distant pressure.

With my head numb, it was safe to proceed with conversation. I told him that I worked on the Unified Model. He told me that he worked on soldiers. *Had* worked. I asked him why he'd left the army.

The dust, he said, damaged my eyes. If you imagine living inside a hoover bag. Don't worry, I can still see which one is your head.

My daughter brought me Hat, to protect my head from the medic. He smiled a formal and shy smile. He had a bone to pick with me, he said. Why can't the military get a good forecast in Afghanistan? I considered saying that I had lied and was just a writer, really. But it was time to take responsibility for all of my lives. Would that be pre-2008? I asked. 2003, he confirmed. You weren't part of the Model then, I said.

While he drew triclosan-coated nylon through my head, I asked if he had children. He didn't reply. I couldn't see his face, so I didn't know if he'd heard me. Eventually he said that in Afghanistan he'd made friends with a thirteen-year-old girl called Saba. Saba used to hang around the ex-Soviet fortress where they were stationed. She was wilful and she was funny; she could mimic English accents. The soldiers laughed but told her to keep outside the perimeter. She told them she could predict the weather, and she could: it turned out that Saba was a more reliable forecaster than the official weather reports.

Saba was our Met Office, he said. We'd be going out on patrol, on a lovely clear day, and Saba would warn us the dust would arrive at such and such a time, and she was always right.

Except one day, when the forecast said it would be stormy and she said, in a Cockney accent, that the forecast was a joke, they trusted her over the forecast. They got caught in a haboob; they did not see the IED.

I wondered if this story was an attack on me, as representative of the failings of the Met Office. Or perhaps he told it to every gashed head, to put our injuries in perspective. Perhaps he was doomed to repeat it. Or perhaps my daughter had stirred in him a new honesty, even with himself. I looked at her, running with scissors between rooms, rolling a glass vase along the floor, emptying the bin.

She will, I have no doubt, bring an end to war. She will break the carbon-military complex. She will save us.

A few nights later, the medic went on, there was a knock on my window. It was Saba. She wanted to say something. She had returned, knowing the dangers, to say something—but was for the first time tongue-tied. I told her I was going to have to detain her unless she left. I told her we were no longer friends. There were men who would kill her if they found her.

She said nothing, she just stood there. But I couldn't do it. I couldn't keep her there and turn her over to the police. I convinced her to leave and never come back.

That was the first time I ever felt like a father, I think, when I told Saba to leave.

It was clear that was the end of the conversation. I let myself enjoy, for a moment, the reassuring spectacle of a large, strong man engaged in gentle work. He put away his things with the same patience as when he had laid them out, disposing of anything that had touched my skin. He declined a cup of tea and left with no evidence of me on his instruments.

I am standing in the poem where you think you're God, my wife said. The one with the luge and the dog and the triathlete. In real life it's freezing.

My groin tingled. She sounded mischievous and uncompromising, a mood I love. I needed a mood I love.

She was at a boutique conference about the future of smallholding, in a central European alpine town that had for a millennium kept the most cutting-edge animal stock: two black bears in a pit in the central square. They looked thin and photographed.

She explained how the landscape was different from the poem, without a father attempting to control the scene with his pen. She said in real life there wasn't any factory dyeing the water red, but she was sure all the men in the bar were actors and the previous night one of them had played the part of a lifeguard and pulled a drunk student out of the water and onto the snow-covered bank.

In real life the lake was a reservoir. An iron beast poked through the silver water's centre: cock of the submerged church. Before it was abandoned and flooded, the hamlet had been famous—seriously—for its sanatorium, which cared for every Napoleon from across the continent. Stones from the building had been used to make the dam, swapping psychic for physical pressure.

My wife had not seen a child in seventy-two hours. It was difficult to get a sense of proportion, she said, without them around. The vanguard farmers looked huge one minute and miniscule the next. My body was on her mind.

I told her I had liberated a swallow from the baby's bedroom.

Again? she said. They left months ago. What's going on?

I told her the river was at 5.8 metres and the flood risk was orange.

What are you hiding? she said.

I had decided my head injury could wait. I had also decided not to worry her with the knowledge that the baby had been vomiting for the last twelve hours, was in fact vomiting right now, on my shoulder, after she had—seriously—eaten four pages of printed text, the first draft.‡

I refused to be worried, which meant that I was worried sick. I thought about phoning my mum but instead conducted an imaginary conversation with her in which I disagreed with everything she said. I took the baby for a walk with the idea that she could be aired: that the plastic and the tar dust could be thinned by the atmosphere passing through.

No one had forced her to eat my words. But what difference was there between allowing her to eat the printed sheets and forcing her to, when she will eat anything that floats down to her while in another room her father is absorbed in reading about the massive, unprecedented precipitation event approaching central Europe?

I filled the silence by telling my wife about my visit to the aquarium. I explained the frightening affinity between child and fish and how I watched our daughter become increasingly frustrated with the glass that separated her from her aquatic home, a frustration she took out on the play area at the end. While the children play, the adults are treated to displays about human destruction. However hard you try to process the terrible facts, they slide out of your brain and into the ball pit, where nothing makes sense but everything is good.

My wife, who knew me well enough not to need to be told what was really going on to know what she should do, said it would be no problem to get an earlier train and plane.

Perhaps that could be good, I said. But I am not asking for help. Remember: I am fine and I am not asking you for help.

A woman slipped over the platform edge. Her guide dog pulled the other way and she landed on her torso, legs over the side. I ran across the wet platform. The woman stood and hissed at her dog. The train pulled in. I helped them on along with my daughter. The carriage was a simple metal room. The heating was forceful and the windows were open to the cold rain. It felt exposed but also homely and also intrepid. The new airport was built on a former military base. The view was of the shapeless wild permitted when humans require camouflage. My daughter crouched and was friendly to the golden retriever's nose. I winked and looked in my bag to see if there was anything I could give to my daughter to express my affection. I had nothing. Bad mother, I thought. I'm a bad mother. When James Brown wants to emphasise his cool he says he's a woman. He says he's a woman not so good with her children. Am I right? I remembered myself and opened my latest distraction, a novel. Gently with the dog, I said, directing the command at the blind woman. She was holding a huge book open on her knees. She ran her fingertips over the paper and rocked her head and moved her lips. She was frowning but it seemed to me a flamboyant celebration of life. Overhanging foliage swept the top of the train. It did not need my belief to sound like baptism. Then the smell of manure.

Teenagers in Santa hats swore and giggled through held noses. The dog sat up and my daughter stared at the blind woman as if her leg was barking. The blind woman would become aware that she was being stared at if I told my daughter not to stare. Instead we named parts of the dog. She spoke gravely, as though the words sank deep into the animal. The dog rested its *head* on its *paws* and I returned to *A Russian Novel* by Emmanuel Carrère. The chapter was a story the author wrote as a love letter to his partner. He explains that he knew she would be taking a train the day the story was published in a newspaper, and so he made sure that she bought it to read on the journey. The story doubles as a set of instructions. He imagines her actions on the train in the hope that his description will come true. He sets the scene, the train pulling out of the station, and then walks her into the full carriage. She reads. She brushes her nipples as she looks out of the window. I could see the writer watching me watch myself. I waited for the warmth to dissipate. You ask new parents and they are relieved to talk about the new sex, the new waiting. But I've never heard anyone talk about *sexuality* after having children. I think I imagined that random arousal would disappear; that it doesn't is both inconvenient and heartening. The blind woman, I could see

in the window, was reading wildly, at a mysterious angle to the beat of the train on the track.
Why should I be embarrassed inside the book?
Submission felt suddenly like defiance. The
story rushed towards La Rochelle. By Niort,
every bathroom on the train is occupied by
a woman who has locked the door, pulled down
her knickers and the dog snapped me out of
the book. My daughter was standing and silent.
She hung her head as if humiliated. I pulled her
up onto the seat and kissed her head. I would
have liked to kick the dog. A voice said, He ok?
Don't worry, I said. The voice said, Is the little
one ok? She's fine, I said, not knowing where to
look. I placed my daughter on the seat next
to the window and looked out. The smell of dog
on my daughter kept the episode lingering.
The train stopped at a station, the teenagers left,
I explained we weren't getting off, my daughter
did not accept my explanation. Did Sherpa
feel irritated? Was he proud of his protective
bark? I was indignant on his behalf. How little
his master seemed to appreciate his dedication.
No wonder he snapped. The train moved us
on. The woman was soon reading again, more
engrossed than before. I wanted a dog to guard
me while I exposed myself to words. My daughter pinched my arm and pointed out a cow I
couldn't see, or saw a cow that wasn't there, or
thought about a cow or felt forming the idea of

a cow, or said a word that sounded like cow, like
ow, the reaction she pinched me in search of,
or her own reaction—now that the thought, if
not the teeth, had sunk in—to the dog's snap,
and I tucked her hair behind her ear and said,
I love you. Low branches swept and bumped
the top of the train. Something fell through the
window. It was a painful sound lying on the
table. Squirrel, my daughter said. I touch it.
There was blood on the table. The smell of pine
disinfectant. The ragged grey and auburn body
uncollected. The dog lost control. The woman,
tied to the leash, slammed into the chair in
front, banging her head, the book on the floor.
The squirrel jumped at the window. My daughter burrowed into the seat. The blind woman
shouted a magic word and her dog remembered its training. Nothing moved except the
squirrel's flexing stomach. It was loosened by
the fall. It was pregnant. It was too early or too
late in the year for a squirrel to be pregnant.
The young conductor had arrived and I told
him the squirrel was pregnant. Acne. The smell
of sore skin. He hovered a few seats away and
muttered about rabies. He messed with his
machine. It does not need a ticket. The dog was
conflicted. The blind woman stood, apologised
again for her outrageous companion and re-
quested, with forceful politeness, to know what
was there. The image shot through her body.

She held her hand to her throat. She said that it must be reassured that we are not a threat. She took a packet of crisps from her bag. The young man announced that we were six minutes from the airport. A pregnant squirrel required us to restrain ourselves for six minutes. Life seemed loosely held together and brief and weird. And then what? I opened the crisps and shook a few onto the novel I had stopped reading. The squirrel flinched. I saw three heartbeats in the loose grey pelt. My daughter gripped my arm and giggled. I whispered, The squirrel is going to eat some crisps. He's had a shock. He's going to feel better. I don't know why the need for a fictional pronoun, except the bruised bones within the womb within the metal train carriage. My daughter became aware she herself could eat the crisps. The squirrel clattered its fingers on the window. I remembered holding hands in A&E after the red square of thick blood. On the train I asked the blind woman quietly, not wanting the animals to hear, what we would do when we got to the station. She said, She'll smell her way outside. Three minutes of life until the airport. The delight so sincere in my daughter's eyes that I thought I would concoct any scene, even this one, to share it with her again. The woman was whispering to her dog. Her dog bore a grin as wide as my daughter's. The pleasure was infectious.

The train slowed. I placed my daughter in the aisle, keeping her hand in mine. I fumbled our large bag. We shrieked, thinking it had crushed the squirrel, but the squirrel was by my feet. By the dog. In the dog.

/

My wife texted to say she was not on the plane. She was on a stationary TGV. They are advising wetsuits, she said, for anyone who wants to get home for Christmas.

I let my daughter take a croissant into the ball pit. I watched the blind woman disappear into advanced airport security. I imagined a controlled explosion of Sherpa.

I dawdled, as though the system might feel sorry for me and produce my wife.

We drifted in and out of shops. My daughter asked if we were going to granny's house last Tuesday. Sometimes the child must take the initiative. We caught the next train to Birmingham.

The following morning, my mother suggested that me and my stepfather go out and get some air. The exclusively male thing is awkward for everyone but I was grateful when he drove the two of us to a small area of protected pools and reeds called the flashes. He comes to look at the birds.

I was dressed in layers of old and other people's clothes. We walked along the slippery boards and were shaded by horizontal snow. My head stitches ached sweetly. I mocked my stepfather's bright technical hat. He suggested I might stop skimming stones on the water.

I answered my phone, thinking it would be my wife. An automated message said the river was at 8 metres and the flood risk was brown.

Somebody is going to get flooded, I thought. I feel sorry for that person.

There were two other men dressed in combat vests in the wooden hide. We opened the shutters to look at the view we had seen from the path, framed by a long, open rectangle. I pretended to knock on the scene and asked,

Is this playing live?

No one laughed.

We looked away from the lake to full feeders strung from branches and a mesh-covered trough piled with stale bread and seeds. This was the only obviously human part of the landscape. It was also the part where all the non-human animals were.

I wanted to ask my stepfather what it had been like to be a father to me as a baby. I have sometimes found myself remembering him there, trapped in my bedroom with a space where the baby would be. I wanted him to tell me that it had been hard but ok. For him to give me that would be trespass.

Something precious about my relationship with him is predicated on the fact that he had *not* been there. I grew up with the privilege of having him as the only higher authority who also deferred to a higher authority. Love can be formal at the same time as absolute—and absolute love can be built step by step, and it cannot. One morning you find it is just there, like a baby's laugh.

When he was a child, the closest my step-father had come to birdwatching was to follow an older boy hunting with a pellet gun around the Lincolnshire docks. But in his teens he had seen a heron while out with Jay. Jay was the uncle of his friend Helen—Helen would become his first wife.

Like all the men in their families, Jay was a docker. He was also a prize shooter, and he knew birds from how they rose up out of the camouflage of a tree or a bush into unprotected air. But he didn't need to point out the heron.

It looks foreign, I said to my stepfather.

Then and now, he agreed.

He told me, quietly, about coming across a heron completely iced over, alive inside, stuck to the ground with frost, bill frozen shut. He said he'd decided to kill it—kill what was alive in it. He said that he had seen its body remembering flight as he approached.

It was only when he was within touching distance that it occurred to him he would have to use his hands. But he stopped himself. Once he'd enjoyed that kind of force, he said, there would be no way back.

A squirrel ran up the leg of the trough, strained its arms towards the nuts, which it couldn't reach; dug the metal into its plump body, still couldn't reach; gave up, ran down the leg again. Flicked its head. Started up the leg again.

It didn't know how lucky it was.

We took it in turns with the binoculars, holding them until our hands shook and returned to our pockets.

I wondered when I was going to tell him that I was not ok—that I was a not-ok father; that every morning I woke beside myself with rage.

I could not tell my stepfather that I was not ok.

I shared my own story about a dying animal. I told him that before he moved in with us, a cat of ours had kittens. One night a Tom came in the cat flap and shook one of them to death. My mother arrived too late. She said she would have killed the Tom with her bare hands.

He suggested we move to another hide. I would tell him that I was not ok on the walk to another hide.

I found the dead kitten, he said. I caught the Tom but it bit my shoulder and I let go. It was your mother who broke the news to you and your sister, in the morning.

We walked on. I wanted to apologise but did not know what for. I kicked a stone off the duckboards into the reeds.

When he stopped to look at a bird I asked him how he had come to know Jay so well, given that he was only the uncle of his first wife, Helen. He lowered the binoculars. Helen lived with her mother's brother and his wife, he told me. Her mother was killed in a car crash when she was very young.

Then he was pointing at the dirty edge of the reeds. It's gone. No, there it is. A long red nose. Blue underside, fat.

We watched it follow the edge of the reeds, jabbing at the ice, until it disappeared.

He smiled.

A water rail, he said.

The name reminded me of *vodka luge*.

When he and Helen were first married,

he worked in a factory poking a pea-washing machine with a long stick when it clogged. The windows had a view of the estuary, where he would watch thousands of wading birds blown off the course of their migrations south. He loved oystercatcher, snipe, avocet and plover sifting the sand, but always hoped for Arctic tern, in the first miles of their flight from one end of the world to the other. They had a taste for the green effluent that flowed from the factory straight into the sea.

It was no longer snowing. We entered a hide overlooking the lake. There was a cheerful family inside and the smell of chicken sandwiches. They washed down their chunks of bird with lids of tea from a dented Thermos.

One of the teenage boys was fiddling with a telescope. He couldn't hide his dismay that his family were only interested in the foreground, where a rat might dash out of its hole again to claim the feeding table from the squirrel. If we were lucky, a hawk might dive down to eat it.

My stepfather looked so peaceful as he watched the brown ones and blue ones and pink ones pick seeds from the feeders. I tried to imagine what they must look like to him. I looked for the bird inside the bird. The bird that wanted to talk about something. The bird that was about to say that it was not ok.

Something grey-blue just below the level
of the hide's windows, up and down and gone.
The family all talked at once.
My stepfather missed it.
I had to admit that it was a thrill.
I pretended to my stepfather that it was not a
thrill. Nothing. Just a smudge.
It was dark. The wire on the duckboards
shone under our feet. I had to let everything
slip. I had to tell him that I was not ok. I had to
tell him that I was not gentle. Tell him about
the desperate want to break
it all and to be broken, break
and be broken,
break
happiness across the rage,
which breathes through what is broken
only when the
breaking is complete,
when breaking
never breaks. It never empties. Step
in milk in socks
and screaming. The father speaks
or no one speaks. A tiny pair of lungs
the model
doesn't take a break to
vacant rage which breaks
into a prison every night. Apologetic rhythm,
shameful breaking boastful
rage that rage

is qualified. The break
that seals
the sorry facts in amber
when he told me he had lost his hat

I laughed out loud, startling something in
the reeds.

He apologised for being so forgetful. He
was annoyed with himself. He did not want
to see himself compromised like this—and
nor did I.

But nor did I want to retrace my steps.

I could not, in fact, turn around.

I could not go back. I had to keep going
forward, wherever it led. I considered the
prospect of going ahead and sitting in the car
and waiting for my stepfather to retrace his
own steps alone.

I felt his hand on my shoulder.

If we are lucky we might see an owl, he said.

The hides were empty. The smell of chicken.
It felt wrong that the views through the windows were still switched on: the birds were just
as busy when no one was looking.

We walked in silence. My mind was formal,
blank.

We found his hat on a post right by the
entrance. There was a large emerald feather

stuck into the lurid technical fabric. He said it was from a heron, matter-of-factly.

You're ok, he said, out of nowhere. We are here together.

In the car he handed me the feather and told me he had a confession to make. It wasn't quite true, what he'd said about his first wife's family. She had always lived with her aunt and uncle because her parents had been too poor to take care of her. It was her aunt that was killed in a car crash, not her mother. But she only came to know that later, before they were married: that her mother, her biological mother, was still alive. He said he didn't know why he had to lie.

Above 8.13 metres the river is no longer in the river. My wife and I met, chest-deep in it, on our doorstep, on Christmas Eve. She kissed the scar on my head and we laughed in the face of misfortune.

We waded into our house holding hands. We waded and steadied one another in the brown current. I picked a chocolate off the floating tree and placed it on my wife's tongue. We stumbled to the staircase and dragged ourselves up the dry steps, stripping off as we climbed to the dry bedroom. We made love among the ruins.

For six drafts that was the truth. But now I am ready to admit that when our house flooded I stayed, even in fiction, with my mother and stepfather. A house full of sewerage is no place for a one-year-old, we agreed.

My wife phoned on Christmas Day. She was crying. She gave the height of the water and the height of the drawer where I stored my laptop and notebooks. I understood precisely what she was telling me and I was confused. I heard her ask someone, in the strange close distance behind a phone, to stop taking photographs of the notebooks she was attempting to unstick from one another in the street. The camera is a Christmas present, I heard the man protest.

In the following days, my wife and her family removed everything from the ground floor of the house which had been earned over

the previous six months: two tables, an arm-
chair, three kitchen chairs, a high chair, a sofa,
a chest of drawers, TV, lamps, pots and pans,
Christmas tree. The miniature hamster furniture: the wheel, the house, the tunnel, the food
dish and the cage itself, which had ended up
in the sink, holding a frog.

They brushed the black mud out of the front
and back doors. They rolled up carpets, with
leeches inside, and threw them out. Dragged
out the washing machine, freezer and dish-
washer. Piled up wet possessions: clothes, toys,
books, alcohol.

A flooded house is full of life, my wife said on
the phone. There are slugs in the fridge, she said.
It's the house-warming party we never had.

Our daughter had been promised her mother
too many times. At night she cried and with no
one to shout at I shouted at my own mother.
My mother had no one to shout at so we made
up—and I booked a train.

/

On seeing the house my daughter said,

> We left pavement outside
> Silly
> The river took it

The water had drained from inside the house.
Outside, the river fed a large oval pool, covering two streets and a children's play area.
The current gathered objects around a lamp-
post. Tree trunks and stones flowed with
cutlery and nappies. Our adjoining neighbour
was flooded, like we were, but the next house
was dry.

By the time my daughter and I arrived there
had been time for us to be shocked by what
we already knew. I stared in disbelief that the
reality was the same as the news.

The house smelt more like the earth than
the earth. The high water mark was lined with
Christmas tree needles. Our daughter played
hide-and-seek with furniture that used to
be there.

My wife took me upstairs and showed me
the watery blue line on the pregnancy test.

I spent the next few days sponging my love
onto walls and floors. One by one I bleached
books, clothes and toys, caressing them tenderly
with the human taint.

Then I changed my mind and threw them
out: possessions were obstacles in the way of
LIFE. The river had done me a favour.

We drove to dry ground to bury the hamsters. My daughter and I and predictive text
co-wrote a speech on my phone:

Have
Had
Hammer
Hamster

which we repeated until it was an elegy that
made us laugh.

At the house, first-person was porous in ways
that the images obscure. We were no longer
sitting in a hide, with nature out there, at the
end of a telescope. There was no clear separation between inside and outside. The front
door was too bloated to close. People came and
went, bringing snow on their shoes and leaving
with slugs in their pockets and zinc on their
fingertips. At the petrol station, just out of shot,
someone was buying flowers from Ethiopia.
Someone was eating or opening a window or
just walking dully along. Everything was on
its way to becoming everything else, and

Please can somebody just give me a form
to fill in.

The notebooks sat in the hallway like a
hideous cake. Life on the paper was nourished
by fertilizer, washed into the river from fields
upstream.

/

I kept expecting to meet the owner of the house I was cleaning. Finally, three people in hi-vis jackets arrived and asked questions from a form they kept apologising for, as you would a bad dog. I replied with my own apologies.

A man spent a morning hosing down the front of the house and when he returned to do the back yard he brought a film crew. He gave up, saying that whatever it was, it was too much, even for him, and phoned someone at the council. He told us he had sixteen thousand people in his online group. The families in social housing, I found out later, had been instructed to wait for an approved council contractor or risk losing their tenancy. They watched their possessions rot in their homes.

/

The Unified Model had predicted the flood, yet it came as a great surprise.

In a warming world, Coleridge is more right than he could have imagined. The baby, exhaling carbon dioxide, *is* the breeze. The rain. The flood.

Terry, the estate agent who sold us the house before it was built, trembled as he crossed the humid threshold, unable to hide his grief. He floated around and whispered apologies and stroked the condensation on the walls until it became depressing and we gave him an excuse to leave.

He noticed the box of wet notebooks. He insisted I let him take them away and dry them out. He did the thing with his hand, bringing it to an emphatic fist above the item, and I was powerless to resist his help.

Something welled up in me as he stood with the box on the doorstep. I felt my unusual experience gave me a lesson to impart. I told him that we had to see it through the baby's eyes: through the baby's eyes nothing was lost, because the baby was attached to nothing except people—nothing except people and one Vietnamese hat—and that was beautiful.

In response, he gave me a number and told me the company would give me a discount on industrial dehumidifiers, if I mentioned his name.

We got used to the roar and hollow heat of the moisture-extraction machines. The walls paled. We emptied buckets of water back into the river.

New Year came and went. We lay on deck-chairs in the baking indoor heat and drank juice from coconuts, wilfully out of step with the rites of the season, a pleasure like neon in daylight.

We attended ad hoc victims' meetings and they were amazing. They would begin with someone's small but real grievance and escalate, until my wife and I had nominated ourselves to lead a delegation to the international climate change negotiations. At some point, stomachs would rumble and the session would close in a collective, bashful stupor, and we would return to discussing gypsum's permeability (how many darcies is too many darcies?), as we walked back to our cars.

My wife pointed out that the meetings were experiments with scale. No single scale seemed appropriate either to explanations or solutions. If someone spoke about the topography of their street, someone else would mention the feeder rivers, upstream. Then someone would bring in El Niño, and someone else China's coal-powered urbanisation. Then we would have nowhere to go except space or God, neither of which would be appropriate, and the whole network of consequences would start again, with photographs of someone's poisoned cat.

We returned to a house naked from the waist down. We waded into the empty corridor holding hands. We waded and steadied one another in the currents of hot air. I picked up the 'to do' list and romantically crossed something off. We stumbled to the staircase and stripped off as we climbed to the dry bedroom, above the watery blue line. We made love among the ruins.

Gradually the visitors stopped visiting and we were left alone, counting ourselves.

Only Terry returned. My wife was attending a local relief group. Our daughter was asleep. Terry and I sat on deckchairs in the kitchen with cups of tea. He had a holdall. For a moment I thought he was coming to stay.

Terry gave me a detailed description of how he was tending to my notebooks. They were strung up on lines above his boiler. He visited regularly to move them around and ensure an even dry.

He said that two notebooks survived. They were diaries written in broken lines. They were about fatherhood.

I got up and fiddled with the camping stove.

If you have lost your novel, you should make *that* your book, Terry said: *Fatherhood*.

I asked Terry what was in his holdall.

Donations, he said, from friends and relatives in Abuja.

A croak came through the monitor. Terry jumped.

The baby was hot, pillow-creased and quietly frantic. She pointed to the door. I carried her through the door.

The baby changed the scene. That happens: a baby arrives and the waters retreat around an awkward social gathering. She is the version of me that does not have to explain itself.

So Terry, I need to feed this one. I've got some pitta, some yoghurt and five cherry tomatoes. Fancy joining?

From his holdall Terry produced a large chocolate cake.

We cut my daughter a slice and she picked up the part that was left: the cake. Terry thought it was the funniest thing. He asked if he could take a photograph. I watched my daughter look after the enormous cake, just on the cusp of posing, and I cried.

I tried to explain how the crying was good.

The flood spoke on my behalf, I said.
My wife and I have a watery blue line.
I am counting myself.

Terry put his hand on my arm and explained that he didn't know what I was talking about but he knew about houses and this was no place to live.

I said that we were the 1 per cent. He picked up a slug and raised his eyebrows. He said that if nothing else we would be doing him a favour—he felt personally responsible, having sold us the house.

I said that it was good for a child to be out-side even when she is inside. He laughed. Then he put the slug back where he had found it, where it seemed to wait, expecting instruction, like me.

I was not ready to act on Terry's advice and give up on the novel that had bled away and corrupted and fed mould. I was not ready to rely on the sallies of poetry I had written in the corners of my family life, and with my daughter's syntax, to build another story about that experience —one that I could live with. The local computer shop employee tried his best to appear for some time as though there was something he could do to retrieve the data from my saturated laptop. He waved sealed packets of off-brand computer parts in my direction. He connected an improbably large desktop to my laptop, as though it was the adult in the room and my piece of equipment would immediately sober up. Computers are not supposed to be physical any more, he seemed to be saying as he waved me plangently out of the shop. It was Andrew, the wonderfully anti-depressed single father, who said that he had heard that there worked at our local library an expert in the restoration of manuscripts. He told me this while he and his daughter scrubbed our front windowsills with toothbrushes. The library was staffed entirely by volunteers. I had got to know some of the library volunteers at rhyme times and also at non-rhyme times, fuzzy, fun afternoons on the hard-wearing carpet and—when I was lucky —the bean bag, colouring in non-colouring-in books and drinking huge lattes and being educated by my daughter about the relativity of time. The volunteers were resilient men and women, impervious and dramatic when reading stories to children. Over the six months that I had been using the library as mine and my daughter's office, where we conducted our most important business, it had sold off a significant proportion of its books at Sunday fairs—to me. Its entire pre-twentieth-century poetry collection, which I haggled down to the price of a baby's cot, was now bloated with floodwater in a skip. The restorer wrote that she would be delighted to take a look at my notebooks and see what could be done. I retrieved the notebooks from Terry, who had been meticulous. Once he had dried them on a line, he had placed them in chronological order in a dishrack. It was the kind of installation our daughter would construct. Her new thing was to burrow into every activity until it resembled a game or a sculpture. Everything was worth repeating. She could be deeply moved by a moment, any moment, experienced for the second time around. At other times, or even at the same times, she could hardly bear her own desire to recreate, so punishing were the rules she was writing as she went along. Today she was happy to improvise: four times she tipped all the dirty washing on top of her own head; four times she tipped herself into the dirty washing.

She considered it a momentous and hilarious morning's work. I had a persistent desire to congratulate the environment on its commitment to certain basic principles, which meant that it had had no choice but to enter my house and rob me of my endeavours. On the other hand, my daughter's performances made me doubt the so-called laws of physics. She made me believe that the pages and pages of intestine-like ink stains in my notebooks were merely a matter of perspective. If I could just find the correct angle at which to look, they would make a higher kind of sense. As we left the house the sky was a satisfied blue; the creamy clouds were decorative. My wife, my daughter and I arrived at the library early. The cramped room was quiet and busy with dutiful volunteers unhooking Christmas. The place was buzzing with the knowledge that people were packing away more than they were packing away: overripe with tales of the flood, which were everyone's to savour for now, but which would soon be old news. The three of us—the three or four of us—were an optimistic unit, soon to stop being news. This morning my wife and I had risked extending an ongoing list of experiences any person entering the world from her uterus had waiting for them. There was a person inside my wife who will one day, we could reasonably hope, hear Glenn

Gould play the *Goldberg Variations*; hum 'Ob-La-Di, Ob-La-Da'. Someone who has yet to be introduced to Frida Kahlo's eyebrows; to Björk singing the love song of a virus; to '12 Times Lionel Messi Surprised the World!' I wept with joy when considering that there was a person inside my wife who might one day read Primo Levi's autobiography as a carbon atom. There was inside my wife a growing collection of carbon atoms that may come to describe itself—as astonished, overwhelmed by beauty. Our daughter, playing her part in organising the world for the human eye's pleasure, was adjusting a very small boy on the library carpet. The boy did not know he was a passenger on our daughter's train. Our daughter was basically ok with the fact that he did not have a valid ticket but she would have preferred it if he had been sitting up straight and not slouching. My mind was divided between the imaginary train journey and the imaginary restoration of my biro marks on paper. The boy did not resist and the third time she propped him against the poof he remained in what looked to me to be the commuter attitude, slumped with his head low with the weight of his inbox. She was not so lenient with me. She asked for and inspected my ticket twelve times before she was satisfied. Neither she nor I had seen the water in the house—only what

the water left behind. We looked for signs that
the flood had entered her mind and found none.
In the weeks since, she had helped us as much
as we had helped her. She made molehills out
of mountains, tipping the dirty laundry on her
own head. She was nice; she caught us off-guard
with appropriate words—sweet phrases about
futures which excited her—and affection for our
friends and family. As for me and my wife, our
intimacies had spread out from the bed across
the day. There is good reason why *intercourse*
is both the most private and public of nouns.
My wife knocked delicately on the window of
the imaginary train—to save us both from our
daughter's wrath—and gave a pep talk preparing
me for disappointment. I do not like preparing
for disappointment. It feels too much like
disappointment. This time, though, my wife
was right. The expert restorer of manuscripts
sat down opposite me on the only table of
the library café. I opened a notebook at random
—for a split-second divided over whether
more worried to display a page where the text
was legible or a page where it was not—and she
replied that the technical term was 'Fucked'.
Her fine silk hijab fell forward as she swore,
revealing the intense logo of a luxury brand.
She fixed the material back over her dark plait
and explained that she could not change wine
back into water. Then she laughed. Then it was

my turn to speak. I did not know what to say. Look at you, she said, storing your most precious possessions where the water could get them. It is as though you were so happy that you wanted to break it down and start again.

The conversation continued for an hour after that and I was at least half of it. But inside I was stuck having a conversation of one sentence: It is as though you were so happy that you wanted to break it down and start again. I hadn't wanted to lose almost everything I had written since my daughter's birth. The water finds the path of least resistance—but it finds nothing and does no searching. It is just temporarily in the wrong place. The river burst its banks and broke into the cells of spreadsheets at the local council. The system is the United Nations and it is the man who jumped in front of you in the queue at the food bank, who didn't quite apologise but explained that he was an out-of-work trampoline instructor, a sad person who could no longer bounce. We might measure ourselves by our collective response to the surfeit of meaninglessness in the world. If the water was a vehicle for human meaning, the particular arrangement of living souls around our small losses was what it meant to me and my wife. Strangers donated brand-new nail-clippers, after pausing to consider our spiky toes. There is no 'we' and it meant everything that we were there together. I didn't want to start again—I wanted to continue in the way that my daughter seemed able to continue, which was to change. I wanted to translate my anger before I threw a chair across a room. I wanted to be with the high windings of sulphur dioxide as much as the low cry of a newborn baby. I wanted to be friends with the woman sitting opposite me and invite her around to our house for a barbeque when our baby was born. Our older daughter would unpack her plastic medical equipment and check everybody's pulse. This stranger would take control of the grill and burn everything and order everyone a takeaway. She would tell us stories about the volunteers at the library. One daughter would fall asleep leaning against a chair attempting to look nonchalant and grown in conversation. The other would lie under a mobile made from pieces of dried notebook. Afterwards my wife and I would sink together into a large dry sofa in an airy room in front of the TV. When a daughter woke in the night, accusatory and inconsolable, I would be with her and wait.

We stayed with Terry and Grace for three weeks. They would allow us to return home, they said, when our front door could close.

From the outside, their house looked like a Tudor mansion; on the inside, a spaceship. We felt contained and strangely free. My only concern was that I found Terry so persuasive that I had to be on my guard. If I wasn't careful, he would inadvertently sell me a change of life every evening over a pint of porter.

I spent my time doing jigsaws with my daughter, phoning tradespeople, moving credit between credit cards, kissing my wife's stomach and transcribing what survived from my notebooks. The loss of the novel would hit me, like Leopold's death, years after the fact. For now it seemed to me spectacular that nature had made an edit.

Terry and Grace played 2Baba from 6.00 a.m. to 6.10 a.m. They danced to make sure they did something together at least once a day.

Isn't that what *you know* is for? I asked Terry. He said since they gave up on the IVF, sex had become complicated.

Terry shared his partner's anger and it troubled him. They were quiet together, often eating their breakfast on opposite sides of the kitchen. It felt as though they were sitting something out, or waiting for the world to catch up. In the meantime there was little to say.

143

Grace took our daughter much more seriously than she took me or my wife.

My hamsters are on holiday, my daughter
told her. But where have they gone? asked
Grace. How did they get to the airport?

At our daughter's bedtime, Grace thanked
her for their conversation, firmly, and took
a bag of chocolate raisins and a scotch to her
home office. Our daughter sat herself outside
the office door and refused to move.

Grace's attention to our daughter made
Terry agitated. We could hear my wife reading
a book about Noah's Ark upstairs.

It is so beautiful, he said, can we go for
a drive?

He needed logs for his wood-burning stove.

The exclusively male thing is awkward
for everyone but I was happy to get out under
the romantic streetlights. I told Terry how
your body changes when you become a father.
You feel more powerful and less in control.
Everything's much more tactile, you have to
communicate without words and negotiate
a completely new kind of intimacy. I told him
about driving my daughter around an island
trying to get her to sleep, how it was a wonderful
memory and also a lesson in what not to do.

It reminds me, I said, of that moment when you do a little dance at how much money is in your account, until you remember you've already spent it.

The petrol station was out of logs. Terry drove us out to the ring road.

Let's go to the source, he said.

Terry was focused on the road, which hadn't changed for at least as long as it takes to get a toddler to sleep.

You get a lot more heat for your money, he said, if you are prepared to drive.

The plantation shop was also closed. We sat in the car in the dark. Terry bounced his head off the steering wheel.

Hey,

I said—in the way I say Hey to my daughter,

Hey, hey.

I wanted to put on some music and I wanted to slap Terry on the back, as though meeting him after a long absence, and I did neither. He opened his window.

The uplift of sound, when inside greets outside. Trees in uniform rows of different heights. Firewood disappointingly alive.

I don't know how to help Grace, Terry said. She does everything. But I feel so angry all the time, like something has been taken away from me. And she feels so angry all the time, like she can't have everything that she has earned. I see the flood in your house and I think *I want that in my house*.

I can't go back, he said.

You're ok, I said. We are here together.

To relieve the men
from
conversation
the dark rustles.
Glove compartment
baby wipes
to shoot
the stranger
is the breeze passed from
sea and hill and wood
to the car to the beard.
It is difficult to feel the beard because
only murderers and the famous
have bodies.
Enemies hide their secrets in their bodies.
You keep in touch with yours by way of orgasm.
Words
return
before sunrise
to clean up the mess.

While I dreamt of a painless birth
my wife prepared,
the baby prepared. The health services
punchline. The sound envelope
delivered the baby
into the tiny patter of the maternal voice.
Same warm folds of baby talk
cradled lucky bacteria
digest milk.

On hearing the first noises
I was
evacuated
into the room.
I wanted to flood
with infant.
I wanted to embarrass the world
with what it is like for an infant.
My secret is
I don't know what the world is like for an infant.

Which is why we listen to music.
I adore
cells [who?] scream to protect
a face
of two felt triangles
and crayon lips. Reckless, pedantic love
sprouts from atmosphere
cut
everywhere with cells. The father
cried
into adulthood
by his child. The word 'no' arrives months
before
the word 'yes'. Later
she takes herself
to the naughty step,
the first pulpit.
The sermon
slips between

those who died in the floods
and those who survived
as though the line was water
on water. My ink
is borrowed milk.

On the drive home
I wanted to enforce
gentleness
without comparison. I wanted to make
a friend
without firing a shot.
Some minor words would be my own.
I want to stay here
over there
with you
gone. Inside me
the animals
don't hurt.
Happy
chastened fathers
note the balls in the pit
are imported from Denmark.
It is unclear how this work should be rewarded.
It is unclear which parts, if any, should be
repeated.

In the evening's quiet kitchen
the parents are full of questions,
after the day inventing answers.

Ludicrous, juicy, unknown thoughts
share the carer
and the one who cares back.
Your bodies float
heavily
on the day, braced
for affection.
I speak instead of my junction off the M1
cuts happiness
like a pair of scissors,
parts screwed together.
Hiccups, for example
I just know that today she is looking for peace.
The objective is to love the animals
back into the trees.

And just when it seems
today will be as sweet and as compromised
as the past,
the infant
storms in.
Busy working
the present,
she loves consequence
and no consequence,
me
and you.
The room relaxes
as she invents the room.
I can let you let me into the garden.

Our parts share the best lines,
gaps,
but end differently, are different people.

We return to the stage
in costume
as ourselves.
[They dance together]
Thank you

† This happened often. Sample phone note: 'Got the shits and baby with u in public yoilet ripping up toilert paper and trying to sqeeuzr it in gap between yr legs. Stand up and almost knock her pver w yr naked crotch.'

‡ Some ingredients: polyester (ground and melted onto the paper), polypropylene wax (for lubrication), high-grade soot (made by burning tar or creosote), silica (melted glass), clay and calcium carbonate.

Acknowledgements: I am grateful to *The White Review* for serialising this book before it was a book. Other parts were published in different forms in *Prac Crit*, *Science Fiction for Survival: An Anthology for Mars*, *The North*, *The Threepenny Review* and *The World Speaking Back to Denise Riley*. Texts commissioned by Jaybird Live Literature have taken on a new life here. A 2015 Northern Writers Award was encouraging. The line 'I counted myself, counted myself again' draws on a line from Oli Hazzard's 'Sonnet'.

( ) (   ) p   prototype
poetry / prose / interdisciplinary projects / anthologies

Creating new possibilities in the publishing of fiction and poetry
through a flexible, interdisciplinary approach and the production
of unique and beautiful books.

Prototype is an independent publisher working across genres
and disciplines, committed to discovering and sharing work that
exists outside the mainstream.

Each publication is unique in its form and presentation, and
the aesthetic of each object is considered critical to its production.

Prototype strives to increase audiences for experimental
writing, as the home for writers and artists whose work requires
a creative vision not offered by mainstream literary publishers.

In its current, evolving form, Prototype consists of 4 strands of
publications:

(type 1 — poetry)
(type 2 — prose)
(type 3 — interdisciplinary projects)
(type 4 — anthologies) including an annual anthology
of new work, *PROTOTYPE*.